Poor Women, Poor Families

The Economic Plight of America's Female-Headed Households

Harrell R. Rodgers, Jr.

M. E. SHARPE, INC.
ARMONK, NEW YORK
LONDON, ENGLAND

Copyright © 1986 by M. E. Sharpe, Inc.

All rights reserved. No part of this book may be reproduced in any
form without written permission from the publisher, M. E. Sharpe, Inc.,
80 Business Park Drive, Armonk, New York 10504

Available in the United Kingdom and Europe from M. E. Sharpe
Publishers, 3 Henrietta Street, London WC2E 8LU.

Library of Congress Cataloging in Publication Data

Rodgers, Jr., Harrell R.

    Poor women, poor families.

    Bibliography: p.
    1. Women heads of households—United States. 2. Women, Poor—
United States. 4. Public welfare—United States. I. Title.

HV51445.R64   1986   362.8′3′0973   86-6449
ISBN 0-87332-372-6
ISBN 0-87332-373-4

Printed in the United States of America

Table of Contents

Acknowledgments

All books are shared enterprises, and this one is no exception. I owe a great debt to all the scholars whose work I rely upon throughout the text. Fortunately, there are many scholars doing excellent work on many of the issues central to this book. I hope this volume fills a few gaps in our knowledge and that it will stimulate more thought, research, and reasoned debate about the critical issues it covers.

Several colleagues read chapters or helped me with methodological problems. To James Stimson, John McIver, and Raymond Duch I want to express my thanks for their assistance and insights. All the data analysis was carried out utilizing a statistical package written by my colleagues James Stimson and George Antunes. The package—Micro Crunch—was designed for personal computers and allowed me the luxury of analyzing my data as much as I pleased without concern about cost, access, or turnaround time. This was a great help. Several of the empirical chapters were delivered as papers at professional conferences. The feedback that I received from fellow panelists and other participants was invaluable, and I would like to thank all of those involved. A few outside reviewers remain anonymous, but I would like to express my thanks for their counsel and support.

Several departmental secretaries helped me type the various versions of the text. To Melodie Najafi, Vane Jones, and Sandra Jackson my sincere thanks. Anita M. O'Brien did an excellent job of editing the book and improved it considerably. Patricia A. Kolb, social sciences editor at M. E. Sharpe, supported this project from its inception and helped greatly in moving it to completion.

My greatest debt remains to my wife, Lynne, who, despite making her living prosecuting criminals, retains an unshakable faith in the basic decency, intelligence, rationality, and future of humanity. Her faith and love inspire me and give me sustenance.

I would like to dedicate this volume to two little girls who do not yet understand the role they play. To Lainie and Lissie, all my love.

Poor Women, Poor Families

Chapter 1

The Increase in Poor Households Headed by Women

The United States—indeed, the entire Western industrial world—is undergoing a major revolution. The revolution is obvious but often subtle in its complexity and impact. Some of its most obvious implications either have gone unnoticed, have been purposefully ignored, or have yet to be fully understood. The revolution is the change that is taking place in women's roles. The changes have been major, with substantial implications for family structures, the economy, the political system, and society in general. The evidence indicates that there will be a great deal more change, with even more substantial consequences.

The Alteration in Women's Status
and Roles

Throughout the twentieth century women have struggled, with considerable success, to alter their status and roles. In the first half of the century women organized to gain such basic rights as the franchise, the right to own property, and standing to sue in a court of law. Hard-won victories in these areas ended women's status as property (Chafe 1972; Freeman 1975; Murphy 1973; Ross 1973; Smith 1979).

In the second, and current, phase of the women's movement, the emphasis is on gaining legal and social equality. This phase has witnessed the large-scale entry of women into the job market. Between 1960 and 1982 the number of women in the work force increased by more than 106 percent. In 1960 women comprised 33.4 percent of the work force. By 1982, 43 percent of the total work force was female. In 1960 about 38 percent of all women were employed. By 1982 almost 53 percent were employed, bringing the female work force up to 48 million.

Not only are more women in the work force, but the marital status of women currently working has also changed. In 1940, 64 percent of all employed women were single, widowed, or divorced. By 1982, single, divorced, and widowed women were even more likely to be in the work force, but married women had increased their participation rate to the extent that they comprised 59 percent of all working women. Since 1980 there have been more families in the United States with both husband and wife working than families with only the husband working (Bureau of the Census 1985, 413).

Increased employment rates have been greatest for women with children. In 1950 only about 20 percent of all women with children were in the labor force, but by 1980 the number had risen to over 50 percent. The largest proportional increase has been among women with children under the age of 6. Between

1950 and 1982 the employment rate for these mothers increased from 14 to 49 percent (Bureau of the Census 1985, 414).

The changes in women's status and roles have been accompanied by greatly increased rates of divorce, marital separation, and out-of-wedlock births. The result is that women in significantly increasing numbers are becoming the heads of households. The Census Bureau distinguishes three types of households:

- *Family household*: two or more related persons living together;
- *Nonfamily household*: two or more unrelated persons of the same or opposite sex living together;
- *Single household*: one adult living alone.

Since the late 1950s the proportion of all three types of households headed by a woman has increased by over 50 percent. By 1984, 16 percent of all households were headed by a woman: 13 percent for whites, 23 percent for those of Spanish origin, and 44 percent for blacks.

Even more importantly, between 1959 and 1984 the number of female-headed families with children increased by 168 percent. The number of male-headed families increased by only 7 percent. In 1984 one of every five families with children under 18 was headed by a woman (see Table 1.1). This included 16 percent of all white families, 25 percent of all Spanish-origin families, and 52 percent of all black families (see Figure 1.1). In 1959 only one in every eleven families with children was female-headed.

The implications of these changes are enormous, and there are credible estimates that this trend will greatly accelerate over the next couple of decades. For example, a congressional committee recently estimated that the number of children under the age of 10 living in female-headed families would in-

Table 1.1

Families with Children by Type, Selected Years, 1959–1984

Year	Total families	Female-headed families	Percent of total	Other families	Percent of total
1984	32,941	6,832	20.7	26,109	79.3
1983	32,723	6,609	20.2	26,114	79.8
1982	32,567	6,397	19.6	26,170	80.4
1981	32,587	6,488	19.9	26,099	80.1
1980	32,772	6,299	19.2	26,473	80.8
1978	31,735	5,837	18.4	25,898	81.6
1977	31,637	5,709	18.0	25,928	82.0
1976	31,430	5,310	16.9	26,120	83.1
1975	31,377	5,119	16.3	26,258	83.7
1974	31,331	4,922	15.7	26,409	84.3
1973	30,997	4,597	14.8	26,400	85.2
1972	30,810	4,322	14.0	26,488	86.0
1971	30,724	4,076	13.3	26,648	86.7
1970	30,071	3,837	12.8	26,243	87.2
1969	29,995	3,384	11.3	26,611	88.7
1968	29,323	3,269	11.1	26,054	88.9
1967	29,032	3,190	11.0	25,842	89.0
1963	28,317	2,833	10.0	25,484	90.0
1959	26,992	2,544	9.4	24,448	90.6

Source: Bureau of the Census. ''Money Income and Poverty Status of Families and Persons in the United States:1984,'' *Current Population Reports*, series P-60, no. 146.

crease by 48 percent between 1980 and 1990. If this estimate is correct, the number of children in such families would increase from 6 million to 8.9 million. This would mean that by 1990 one of every four children under 10 would live in a family headed by a single woman (Select Committee on Children, Youth and Families [SCCYF] 1983, iv and 27).

The Feminization of Poverty

Although women's roles have been changing very significant-ly, public policies clearly have not kept pace with these changes. The consequences are reflected in part by the crisis

Figure 1.1   **Familes with Children Headed by a Female, 1984**

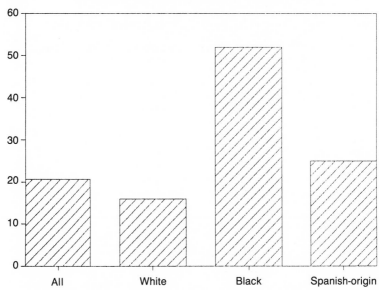

Source: Bureau of the Census, "Money Income and Poverty Status of Families and Persons in the United States: 1984," *Current Population Reports*, series P-60, no. 149.

that currently faces millions of female household heads and their dependents. Since the mid-1970s both the popular press and scholarly journals have become increasingly aware of a new social problem often labeled the "feminization of poverty" (Burlage 1978; Cooney 1979; Pearce 1978). The term refers to the growing percentage of all poor Americans who are women and their dependents. Recent increases in the proportion of all poor living in female-headed families or households have been so dramatic that in 1981 the president's National Advisory Council on Economic Opportunity declared that "All other things being equal, if the proportion of the poor in female-householder families were to continue to increase at the same rate as it did from 1967 to 1978, the poverty population would be composed solely of women and their children before the year 2000."

Table 1.2

Poverty Schedule: Family of Four (Nonfarm), 1959–1984

Year	Standard	Millions of poor	% of total pop.
1959	$2,973	39.5	22.0
1960	3,022	39.9	22.0
1961	3,054	39.9	22.0
1962	3,089	38.6	21.0
1963	3,128	36.4	19.0
1964	3,169	36.1	19.0
1965	3,223	33.2	17.0
1966	3,317	30.4	16.0
1966*	3,317	28.5	15.0
1967	3,410	27.8	14.0
1968	3,553	25.4	13.0
1969	3,743	24.1	12.0
1970	3,968	25.4	13.0
1971	4,137	24.1	11.0
1972	4,275	25.4	12.0
1973	4,540	23.0	11.5
1974	5,038	24.3	12.0
1974*	5,038	24.3	11.5
1975	5,500	25.9	12.0
1976	5,815	25.0	12.0
1977	6,200	24.7	12.0
1978	6,662	24.7	11.4
1979	7,412	26.1	11.7
1980	8,414	29.3	13.0
1981	9,287	31.8	14.0
1982	9,862	34.4	15.0
1983	10,178	35.3	15.2
1984	10,609	33.7	14.4

Source: Derived from U.S. Bureau of the Census, ''Money Income and Poverty Status of Families in the United States,'' series P-60, various years.

*Revision in census calculations.

Figure 1.2   **Poor in Female-Headed Households**

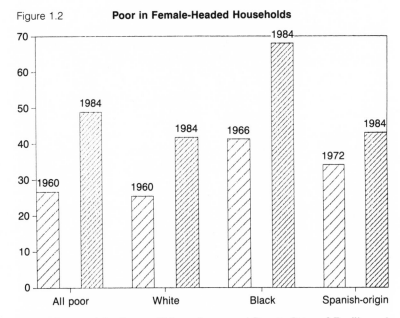

Source: Bureau of the Census, "Money Income and Poverty Status of Families and Persons in the United States: 1984," *Current Population Reports,* series P-60, no. 149.

It is doubtful that anyone actually expects all other things to remain equal, but the rising poverty among women has been so significant that over the last decade women and their dependents have become the major poverty group in America. By the early 1980s almost half of the more than 30 million poor in America were women and their dependent children (see Table 1.2).

Figure 1.2 shows the huge increase that occurred between 1960 and 1984 in the percentage of all the poor who live in households headed by a woman. In 1960 about 27 percent of all the poor lived in female-headed households.[1] Despite the fact

1. The quality of the Social Security Administration's data for the years 1959 to 1964 is somewhat suspect. These data were retrospective, and some of the differences between late 1959 and the early 1960s may reflect collection and reporting problems. For a more in-depth analysis of these problems see Rodgers 1978, and Rodgers 1982, 14–27.

that women head only 16 percent of all households and 21 percent of all families with children, by 1984 over 49 percent of all the poor lived in female-headed households. The change has been substantial for poor whites but even greater for minorities. In 1984, 68 percent of the black poor lived in female-headed households, as did 43 percent of all poor of Spanish origin.

As the next chapter will detail, a critical factor in the feminization of poverty has been the enormous increase in the percentage of all households headed by women. As women head more households poverty increases because female-headed households have exceptionally high rates of poverty. In 1984, for example, only 6.9 percent of all married couple families fell below the poverty line. The poverty rate for female-headed households was five times greater at over 34.5 percent. The rate for white female-headed households was very high (about 27 percent), but for black and Spanish origin female-headed households it was over 50 percent (see Table 1.3).

Poverty among Children

One of the most ominous consequences of the high rates of poverty for women who head families is the deprivation brought to their dependent children. As more and more women have fallen below the poverty level, poverty rates among children have increased very significantly. Since 1982 more than 21 percent of all children under 18 have lived below the poverty level. This is the highest rate of poverty for children since the early 1960s. *One in five children in America now lives in poverty*. This includes over 16 percent of all white children, 39 percent of all children of Spanish origin, and over 46 percent all black children.

More than half of all the poor children in America now live in female-headed families, compared to the 25 percent who did so in the late 1950s and early 1960s (see Figure 1.3). In 1984

Figure 1.3   **Poor Children in Female-Headed Households**

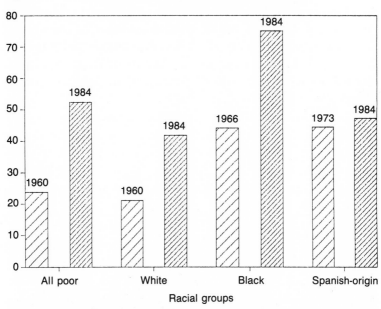

Source: Bureau of the Census, "Money Income and Poverty Status of Families and Persons in the United States: 1984," *Current Population Reports*, series P-60, no. 149.

there were 6.8 million poor children living in female-headed families, representing a 63 percent increase since 1959. By the 1970s an average of 53 percent of all poor children in America lived in female-headed families, with a high of 58.5 percent in 1978. The average for 1980-84 was 51.7 percent.

The poverty rate for children in female-headed families has remained over 50 percent in every year since 1959 except one (in 1979 it was 48.6 percent) (Bureau of the Census 1985, 21). A recent congressional study (Committee on Ways and Means 1985, 7) estimated that if "the proportion of children in female-headed families had not increased during the past 25 years, . . . the number of poor children in 1983 might have been . . . 22 percent lower." A 22 percent reduction in poverty among children would lower the count by about 3 million.

Table 1.3

Poverty Rate for Families, by Type of Family, Race, and Spanish Origin,* 1959–1984

Year	All families				Families with female householder, no husband present				All other families			
	All races	White	Black	Spanish origin	All races	White	Black	Spanish origin	All races	White	Black	Spanish origin
1984	11.6	9.1	30.9	25.2	34.5	27.1	51.7	53.4	7.2	6.4	14.7	16.7
1983	12.3	9.7	32.4	26.3	36.0	28.3	53.8	53.5	7.8	7.0	16.2	18.1
1982	12.2	9.6	33.0	27.2	36.3	27.9	56.2	55.4	7.9	7.0	16.4	18.9
1981	11.2	8.8	30.8	24.0	34.6	27.4	52.9	53.2	7.0	6.3	15.6	15.4
1980	10.3	8.0	28.9	23.2	32.7	25.7	49.4	51.3	6.3	5.6	14.3	15.4
1979	9.2	6.9	27.8	20.3	30.4	22.3	49.4	49.2	5.5	4.8	13.2	13.0
1978	9.1	6.9	27.5	20.4	31.4	23.5	50.6	53.1	5.3	4.7	11.8	12.4
1977	9.3	7.0	28.2	21.4	31.7	24.0	51.0	53.6	5.5	4.8	13.5	13.2
1976	9.4	7.1	27.9	23.1	33.0	25.2	52.2	53.1	5.6	4.9	13.5	15.6
1975	9.7	7.7	27.1	25.1	32.5	25.9	50.1	53.6	6.2	5.5	14.2	17.6
1974	8.8	6.8	26.9	21.2	32.1	24.8	52.2	49.6	5.4	4.7	13.2	14.7
1974†	9.2	7.0	27.8	21.3	32.5	24.9	52.8	49.6	5.7	4.9	14.2	14.7

Year												
1973	8.8	6.6	28.1	19.8	32.2	24.5	52.7	51.4	5.5	4.6	15.4	13.1
1972	9.3	7.1	29.0	(NA)	32.7	24.3	53.3	(NA)	6.1	5.3	16.2	(NA)
1971	10.0	7.9	28.8	(NA)	33.9	26.5	53.5	(NA)	6.8	5.9	17.2	(NA)
1970	10.1	8.0	29.5	(NA)	32.5	25.0	54.3	(NA)	7.2	6.2	18.6	(NA)
1969	9.7	7.7	27.9	(NA)	32.7	25.7	53.3	(NA)	6.9	6.0	17.9	(NA)
1968	10.0	8.0	29.4	(NA)	32.3	25.2	53.2	(NA)	7.3	6.3	19.9	(NA)
1967	11.4	9.0	33.9	(NA)	33.3	25.9	56.3	(NA)	8.7	7.4	25.3	(NA)
1966	11.8	9.3	35.5	(NA)	33.1	25.7	59.2	(NA)	9.3	7.7	27.6	(NA)
1966†	12.7	10.2	(NA)	(NA)	35.1	27.8	(NA)	(NA)	10.0	8.4	(NA)	(NA)
1965	13.9	11.1	(NA)	(NA)	38.4	31.0	(NA)	(NA)	11.1	9.2	(NA)	(NA)
1964	15.0	12.2	(NA)	(NA)	36.4	29.0	(NA)	(NA)	12.5	10.5	(NA)	(NA)
1963	15.9	12.8	(NA)	(NA)	40.4	31.4	(NA)	(NA)	13.1	11.0	(NA)	(NA)
1962	17.2	13.9	(NA)	(NA)	42.9	33.9	(NA)	(NA)	14.3	12.0	(NA)	(NA)
1961	18.1	14.8	(NA)	(NA)	42.1	33.5	(NA)	(NA)	15.4	13.1	(NA)	(NA)
1960	18.1	14.9	(NA)	(NA)	42.4	34.0	(NA)	(NA)	15.4	13.0	(NA)	(NA)
1959	18.5	15.2	48.1	(NA)	42.6	34.8	65.4	(NA)	15.8	13.3	43.3	(NA)

*Persons of Spanish origin may be of any race.
†Based on revised methodology.

Source: Bureau of the Census, "Money Income and Poverty Status of Families and Persons in the United States," Current Population Reports, series P-60, various years.

In summary, women increasingly head households and these households have very high rates of poverty. This is particularly true among minority populations. The poverty that afflicts women has dramatically increased the rate of poverty among children. By 1983 much of the progress made during the late 1960s and throughout the 1970s in alleviating poverty among children had been reversed.

Public Assistance

Not only are women and their dependent children the single largest group of poor in America, they are also the major welfare recipient group (Bureau of the Census 1984a, 1–5). Female family heads and their dependents constitute over 80 percent of all AFDC (Aid to Families with Dependent Children) recipients, over half of all Food Stamp households, almost half of the recipients of free or reduced-price school meals, 55 percent of the households receiving Medicaid, and well over half of the nonaged residents of public housing. The problems that increasingly befall women, in other words, impose very significant costs on society.

Nevertheless, as later chapters will detail, most needy female-headed households either do not receive assistance, or the assistance they do receive does a very poor job of meeting their needs. The vast majority of all AFDC families remain far below the poverty level, and most are still poor when they leave the rolls. This is generally true even when the family receives or has received benefits from more than one welfare program.

In addition, many women originally become poor or economically threatened because of deficiencies in public or private-sector policies.

If women and their children are to be prevented from falling into poverty or to be helped out of poverty, welfare assistance, other social programs and policies, and benefits extended by private employers will have to be significantly reformed and integrated into a much healthier and fairer economic system (Chafetz 1984).

The Organization of This Book

The chapters that follow attempt to dissect the problem of increasing poverty among women and their children. They detail the growth of poverty in female households; identify its most obvious causes and consequences; critique existing welfare, social, and private-sector programs; evaluate policy alternatives; and put forward some practical nonwelfare and welfare solutions. Chapter 2 begins by providing an empirical analysis of the changes in the poverty population over the last two decades that have produced the feminization of poverty. The chapter addresses the major questions about the feminization of poverty raised in the extant literature and provides an in-depth statistical analysis of the impact of women's poverty on children. Chapter 3 addresses the question of why women are increasingly the heads of families and delineates the major causes of poverty among women. Chapter 4 shows why welfare programs neither prevent poverty nor adequately meet the needs of poor women and their dependents. Chapter 5 reviews social welfare programs for women in major Western European nations. The intent here is to provide insights into some innovative programs and experiments in other nations to inform a discussion of reforms of American programs. Finally, Chapter 6 discusses nonwelfare and welfare reforms that would ameliorate the growing problem of poverty among women and their dependents.

Chapter 2

The Feminization of Poverty: A Statistical Overview

In this chapter data will be presented to detail, by racial group, the dramatic increase in the proportion of all the poor who are women and children. The data are then used to examine why this change has occurred. The analysis reveals that the key factor in explaining the rising proportion of women and children among all the poor is not the increasing rate of poverty for women and children or, generally speaking, the decreasing rate of poverty for two-parent families.[1] Instead, it is the huge increase in households headed by women.

Female-headed households suffer a high but steady rate of poverty. As the proportion of all such households has grown,

---

1. An important caveat should be noted. The rate of poverty for all groups is determined by the Social Security Administration's calculation of the official poverty standard. This standard was first calculated in 1965 and then backdated to 1959. Since 1969 the standard has been adjusted yearly according to changes in the Consumer Price Index. The

their high but constant rate of poverty has encompassed larger and larger numbers of poor women and children. Poverty, in other words, has become a matter not just of economics, but also of family structure.

The Increase in Poor Female Heads of Households

The number of poor Americans living in female-headed families has increased dramatically since the 1960s (Figure 1.2). Table 2.1 shows the increase between 1959 and 1984 in the number of poor family and nonfamily households (excluding single households) headed by women (Cooney 1979; Cutright 1974; Lantz, Martin, and O'Hara 1977; Sweet 1972). In 1959 the number of poor female family heads was 1.9 million; by 1984 the figure had jumped 83 percent, to 3.5 million. In 1960 only 24 percent of all poor families were headed by a woman. By 1984 the percentage had increased to over 48 percent. The change has been significant for both white and black families. The 20 percent of all poor white families headed by a female in 1960 rose to 38 percent by 1984. For poor black families, 42 percent were headed by a single woman in 1960, but 73 percent in 1984. Women headed about the same proportion of poor Spanish-origin families in 1984 as in 1973—almost half.

Both the number and proportion of all the poor living in single, family, and nonfamily female households also increased significantly over the last two decades (see Table 2.2). In 1959 there were 10.3 million poor people in female-headed

---

yearly adjustments have been so low that the poverty standard has become an increasingly smaller proportion of median family income. For example, in 1959 the poverty standard for an urban family of four equalled 53 percent of median family income for an urban family of four. By 1980 the ratio for this family size had fallen to 40 percent. Thus, the recent stability of the poverty rate for female-headed families in part reflects the failure of the poverty standard to maintain its historic relationship to median incomes.

Table 2.1

Poor Female Family Heads (No Husband Present), by Race

	Total	Poverty rate	White	Poverty rate	Black	Poverty rate	Spanish-origin	Poverty rate
1984	3,498	,34.5	1,878	27.1	1,533	51.7	483	53.4
1983	3,572	35.8	1,935	28.7	1,541	53.7	455	52.9
1982	3,434	36.3	1,813	27.9	1,535	56.2	425	55.4
1981	3,252	34.6	1,814	27.4	1,377	52.9	399	53.2
1980	2,972	32.7	1,609	25.7	1,301	49.4	362	51.3
1979	2,645	30.4	1,350	22.3	1,234	45.4	300	49.2
1978	2,654	31.4	1,391	23.5	1,208	50.6	288	53.1
1977	2,610	31.7	1,400	24.0	1,162	51.0	301	53.6
1976	2,543	33.0	1,379	25.2	1,122	52.2	275	53.1
1975	2,430	32.5	1,394	25.9	1,004	50.1	279	53.6
1974	2,324	32.1	1,289	24.8	1,010	52.2	229	49.6
1973	2,193	32.2	1,190	24.5	974	52.7	211	51.4
1972	2,158	32.7	1,135	24.3	972	53.3		
1971	2,100	33.9	1,191	26.5	879	53.5		
1970	1,951	32.5	1,102	25.0	834	54.3		
1969	1,827	32.7	1,069	25.7	737	53.3		
1968	1,755	32.3	1,021	25.2	706	53.2		
1967	1,774	33.3	1,037	25.9	716	56.3		
1966	1,721	33.1	1,036	25.7	674	59.2		
1965	1,916	38.4	1,196	31.0	NA			
1960	1,955	42.4	1,252	34.0	NA			
1959	1,916		1,233		551			
Percentage increase	83%		52%		178%		129%	

Source: Bureau of the Census (1985) ''Money Income and Poverty Status of Families and Persons in the United States.'' *Current Population Reports*, series P-60, no. 149, pp. 21–22.

households. By 1984 the number stood at 16.4 million, an increase of 58 percent. About half of the increase occurred in the late 1970s and early 1980s.

The magnitude of these increases is indicated by the fact that in 1960 only 27 percent of all the poor lived in female-headed households. The percentage increased steadily until the mid-

1970s, when half of all the poor in America lived in female-headed households. In 1978 the percentage reached 52.6 percent, but great increases in poverty for all household types in the 1980s reduced the percentage of the poor in female-headed units to 48 percent in 1984.

Variations by Race

Figures for the poverty rate (the percentage of all people of a given type living below the poverty line) for members of female-headed households, broken down by race, are quite revealing (see Table 2.2). The rate of poverty for members of female-headed households actually declined from a high of 50.2 percent in 1959 to 34 percent in 1984 (see note 1). During the 1970s the rate of poverty for female-headed households averaged 35 percent, very similar to the average so far during the 1980s. The rate varies considerably, however, by race.

White Poor. White households have the lowest rate of poverty and have had the smallest percentage increase in poverty. These findings should not obscure the fact that the rate of poverty for white female-headed households is still high. Between 1970 and 1984 the poverty rate for such households averaged 27.6 percent. The number of poor in white families grew by over 2 million people between 1959 and 1984 (to over 9 million), an increase of 34 percent. Between 1970 and 1984 an average of 48.7 percent of all white poor Americans lived in female-headed households. Poverty, then, is clearly a very serious problem for white households headed by women.

Black Poor. The figures for black female-headed households are staggering (Bianchi and Farley 1979; National Black Child Development Institute 1980). The number of poor in such households increased by 122 percent between 1959 and

Table 2.2

Poor in Female-headed Households (No Husband Present), by Race

Year	All persons	Poverty rate	Percent of all poor	White	Poverty rate	Percent of all poor	Percent of all white poor
1984	16,440	34.5	48.0	9,570	27.3	28.0	41.0
1983	16,848	36.1	47.4	9,768	28.5	27.5	40.4
1982	16,336	36.2	47.5	9,392	28.7	27.3	39.8
1981	15,738	35.2	49.4	9,347	28.4	29.4	43.4
1980	14,649	33.8	50.0	8,569	27.1	29.3	43.5
1979	13,503	32.0	51.8	7,653	24.9	29.3	44.4
1978	12,880	32.3	52.6	7,262	24.9	29.6	44.6
1977	12,624	32.8	51.5	7,221	25.5	29.2	44.0
1976	12,586	34.4	50.4	7,356	27.3	29.4	44.0
1975	12,268	34.6	47.4	7,324	28.1	28.3	41.2
1974	11,469	33.6	49.0	6,673	26.5	28.5	42.2
1973	11,357	34.9	49.4	6,642	27.9	28.9	43.8
1972	11,587	36.9	47.4	6,682	25.4	27.3	41.2
1971	11,409	38.0	44.6	7,146	32.2	27.9	40.2
1970	11,154	38.2	43.9	6,832	31.4	26.8	39.0
1969	10,412	38.4	43.1	6,531	32.1	27.0	39.2
1968	10,364	38.9	40.8	6,400	32.3	25.2	36.8
1967	10,591	40.6	38.1	6,600	33.9	23.7	34.8
1966	10,250	41.0	35.9	6,511	33.9	22.8	33.7
1965	11,058	46.0	33.3	7,085	38.5	21.3	31.5
1960	10,663	49.5	26.7	7,207	42.3	18.1	25.4
1959	10,390	50.2	26.3	7,115	43.8	18.0	25.0
Percent increase	57.2%				36.1%		

Source: Bureau of the Census (1985) ''Money Income and Poverty Status of Families and Persons in the United States: 1984'' (Advance Data from the March 1984 Current Population Survey), *Current Population Reports*, series P-60, no. 149, p. 22.

Year	Black	Poverty rate	Percent of all poor	Percent of all black poor	Spanish origin	Poverty rate	Percent of all poor	Percent of all Spanish-origin poor
1984	6,462	52.9	19.0	68.0	2,068	54.3	6.0	43.0
1983	6,643	56.0	18.7	67.2	1,944	53.3	5.5	41.9
1982	6,533	57.4	18.9	67.4	1,849	57.4	5.3	42.9
1981	6,081	55.8	19.1	66.3	1,682	54.0	5.3	45.3
1980	5,807	53.1	19.8	67.7	1,501	52.5	5.1	43.0
1979	5,571	52.2	21.4	69.2	1,241	48.9	4.7	42.5
1978	5,392	53.1	22.0	70.7	1,158	53.3	4.7	44.4
1977	5,230	53.9	21.1	67.7	1,204	53.3	4.9	44.6
1976	5,024	54.7	20.1	66.1	1,144	54.3	4.6	41.1
1975	4,784	53.6	18.5	63.4	1,189	55.6	4.6	39.7
1974	4,705	54.3	20.1	65.5	1,012	51.4	4.3	39.3
1973	4,564	55.4	19.9	61.8	917	55.5	4.0	38.7
1972	4,670	57.3	19.1	60.6	822	51.5	3.4	34.0
1971	4,129	55.8	16.1	55.8				
1970	4,213	55.8	16.6	55.8				
1969	3,766	57.8	15.6	53.1				
1968	3,807	58.6	15.0	50.0				
1967	3,892	61.6	14.0	45.8				
1966	3,657	65.2	12.8	41.2				
1959	2,906	70.0	7.3	36.8				

Percent
increase 125%   125%

Table 2.3

Poor in Female-headed Families (No Husband Present), by Race

Year	All persons	Poverty rate	Percent of all poor	White	Poverty rate	Percent of all poor	Percent of white poor
1984	11,831	38.4	35.1	5,866	29.7	17.4	25.5
1983	12,101	40.3	34.1	6,046	31.4	17.0	25.0
1982	11,701	40.6	34.0	5,686	30.9	16.5	24.2
1981	11,051	38.7	34.7	5,600	29.8	17.6	26.0
1980	10,120	36.7	34.6	4,940	28.0	16.9	25.1
1979	9,400	34.9	36.0	4,375	25.2	16.8	25.4
1978	9,269	35.6	37.8	4,371	25.9	17.8	26.9
1977	9,205	36.2	37.5	4,474	26.8	18.1	27.2
1976	9,029	27.3	36.1	4,463	28.0	17.9	26.7
1975	8,846	37.5	34.2	4,577	29.4	17.7	25.7
1974	8,462	36.5	36.2	4,278	27.7	18.3	27.2
1973	8,178	37.5	35.6	4,003	28.0	17.9	26.4
1972	8,114	38.2	33.2	3,770	27.4	15.4	23.3
1971	7,797	38.7	30.5	4,099	30.4	16.0	23.0
1970	7,503	38.1	29.5	3,761	28.4	14.8	21.5
1969	6,879	38.2	28.4	3,577	29.1	19.8	21.5
1968	6,990	38.7	27.3	3,551	29.1	19.0	20.4
1967	6,898	38.8	24.8	3,453	28.5	12.4	18.2
1966	6,861	39.8	24.1	3,646	29.7	12.8	18.9
1965	7,524	46.0	22.7	4,092	35.4	12.3	18.2
1960	7,247	48.9	18.2	4,296	39.0	10.8	15.2
1959	7,014	49.4	17.8	4,232	40.2	10.7	14.8

Source: Bureau of the Census (1985) ''Money Income and Poverty Status of Families and Persons in the United States: 1984'' (Advance Data from the March 1985 Current Population Survey), *Current Population Reports*, series P-60, no. 149, p. 22.

1984. In 1984, 68 percent of all poor black Americans lived in female-headed households. As with white households, the rate of poverty among black households has not changed significantly. Between 1966 and 1984 the rate of poverty for black female-headed households averaged 56 percent, with only moderate variation.

Spanish-Origin Poor. Accurate figures for Spanish-origin citizens have been compiled only since 1972, but those that are available are instructive (Table 2.2). The number of poor citi-

Year	Black	Poverty rate	Percent of all poor	Percent of all black	Spanish-origin	Poverty rate	Percent of all poor	Percent of all Spanish-origin poor
1984	5,666	54.6	16.8	59.7	1,764	56.2	5.2	36.7
1983	5,736	57.0	16.1	58.0	1,672	55.1	4.7	36.0
1982	5,698	58.8	16.6	58.7	1,601	60.1	4.6	37.2
1981	5,222	56.7	16.4	56.9	1,465	55.9	4.6	39.4
1980	4,984	53.4	17.0	58.1	1,319	54.5	4.5	37.8
1979	4,816	53.1	18.5	59.8	1,053	51.2	4.0	36.0
1978	4,712	54.2	19.2	61.8	1,024	56.4	4.2	39.3
1977	4,595	55.3	18.6	59.5	1,077	56.7	4.3	39.9
1976	4,415	55.7	17.7	58.1	1,000	56.6	4.0	35.9
1975	4,168	54.3	16.1	55.2	1,053	57.2	4.1	35.2
1974	4,116	55.0	17.6	57.3	915	53.1	3.9	35.5
1973	4,064	56.5	17.7	55.0	881	57.4	3.8	37.2
1972	4,139	58.1	16.9	53.7				
1971	3,587	56.1	14.0	48.5				
1970	3,656	58.7	14.4	48.4				
1969	3,225	58.2	13.3	45.4				
1968	3,312	58.9	13.0	43.5				
1967	3,362	61.6	12.1	39.6				
1966	3,160	65.3	11.1	35.6				
1959	2,416	70.6	6.1	24.3				

zens in these female-headed households increased by 151 percent between 1972 and 1984. As with other female-headed households the rate of poverty changed little (the yearly average was 53.4 percent with modest variations), but the number of poor increased significantly. Between 1980 and 1984 an average of 43 percent of all the Spanish-origin poor lived in female-headed households.

Table 2.3 continues this analysis by focusing just on female-headed families (i.e., two or more related persons living together). The data reinforce the analysis above. The number of poor in female-headed families increased from 7 million in 1959 to 11 million in 1984, growing steadily between 1969 and 1981 but stabilizing since 1982. The numbers increased significantly during the 1970s despite the fact that the poverty rate for female-headed families was not increasing. The poverty rate for female-headed families increased quite rapidly during the 1960s, but it basically stabilized during the 1970s and 1980s. This again indicates that the number of poor in female-headed families increased rapidly in the 1970s because the base of such families was growing. More female-headed families produced more poor despite a stabilized poverty rate.

Contrasting tables 2.2 and 2.3 provides another insight into the composition of poverty in female-headed households. Most of the poor in female-headed households are in families. For example, in 1984, 72 percent were in families. This included 61 percent for whites, 85 percent for Spanish origin, and 88 percent for blacks. The feminization of poverty, in other words, is mostly the result of increasing poverty among women and their dependent children.

Changes in Poverty Rate, by Race and Sex

Although the data above clearly show great increases in poor female-headed households, one critical question is not addressed: Could the feminization of poverty be the result of reductions in two-parent or male-headed households living in poverty? In other words, if other types of households have left the poverty ranks, could the number of female-headed households in poverty be the result of their being left behind? Interestingly, the answer varies by race.

White Households. For whites the answer is no. Since 1966 there have not been great reductions in the proportion of white two-parent or male-headed families living in poverty. In

1966 the combined poverty rate for such families was 8 percent; in 1984 it was 7.5 percent. Numerically there were 11.8 million poor in such families in 1966, and 11.4 million in 1984. The poverty rate for one subset of these families—male-headed with no wife present—has increased in recent years. The number of these families is quite small (a total of only 292,000 of all races in 1984). In 1978 the poverty rate for white families of this type was 7.3 percent. In 1984 it was 10.4 percent.

The poverty rate for white female-headed households has not changed much over the years. It was 25.7 percent in 1966 and 27.1 percent in 1984. What has changed is the base of white female-headed households. In 1965 there were 3.9 million such households. By 1984 there were 6.9 million (see Table 2.4). Thus, while the poverty rate for these households has changed little, the rising base has produced a great many more poor white female-headed households: the increase was from 1.2 million in 1959 to 1.9 million in 1984, or 52 percent (Table 2.1). Thus for whites the feminization of poverty is the result of increases in the number of female-headed households, and a persistently high, but rather level, rate of poverty.

Black Households. For blacks, two general factors account for the feminization of poverty. First, there has been a reduction in the poverty rate for black two-parent families. In 1966, 33 percent of all such families were poor. By 1984 the poverty rate for these families had dropped to 13.8 percent. Over this same period the number of poor in black two-parent families decreased by some 50 percent. As with whites, the small group of black male-headed families with no wife present seems to have become poorer in recent years. In 1978 the poverty rate for these 48,000 families was 17.7 percent. By 1984 the number of such families had grown (82,000), and the poverty rate had increased to 23.8 percent.

During the period 1966 to 1984 the poverty rate for black

Table 2.4

Female-headed Households (No Husband Present)

	All F-H house-holds	Percent of all families	White F-H house-holds	Percent of all white families	Black F-H house-holds	Percent of all black families	Spanish-origin F-H house-holds	Percent of Spanish-origin families
1984	10,129	16.0	6,941	12.0	2,964	43.0	905	22.0
1983	9,878	15.9	6,784	12.6	2,874	43.0	810	22.7
1982	9,469	15.4	6,507	12.2	2,734	41.9	767	22.8
1981	9,403	15.4	6,620	12.4	2,605	40.6	750	22.7
1980	9,082	15.1	6,266	11.9	2,634	41.7	706	21.8
1979	8,530	14.6	5,952	11.6	2,430	40.2	570	20.2
1978	8,458	14.6	5,918	11.6	2,390	40.5	542	19.7
1977	8,236	14.4	5,828	11.5	2,277	39.2	561	20.2
1976	7,713	13.6	5,467	10.9	2,151	37.1	517	20.2
1975	7,482	13.3	5,380	10.8	2,004	35.9	522	20.9
1974	7,230	13.0	5,208	10.5	1,934	35.2	462	18.7
1973	6,607	12.2	4,672	9.6	1,822	34.6	386	16.7
1972	6,191	11.6	4,489	9.4	1,642	31.8	355	17.3
1971	5,550	11.1	4,386	9.4	1,506	30.6	329	16.8
1970	5,591	10.8	4,165	9.6	1,382	28.3	—	—
1969	5,439	10.8	4,053	8.9	1,327	28.6	—	—
1965	5,006	10.5	3,882	9.0	1,125	23.7	—	—
1960	4,494	10.0	3,547	8.7	947	22.4	—	—

Source: Bureau of the Census, ''Money Income and Poverty Status of Families and Persons in the United States,'' *Current Population Reports*, series P-60, various years.

female-headed households changed significantly (65.1 percent in 1966; 51.7 percent in 1984), but the number of such households increased even more dramatically. In 1959 there were 947,000 black female-headed households; by 1984 there were about 3 million (Table 2.4). In the 1970s alone, the number of black female-headed households doubled. This increase, and a poverty rate averaging over 50 percent, raised the number of poor female family heads from 551,000 in 1959 to 1.5 million in 1984, or 180 percent (see Table 2.1). Thus, for black households, the feminization of poverty has been caused by a great increase in female-headed households, a high and persistent rate of poverty for such units, and a reduction in the poverty rate for two-parent black families.

Spanish-Origin Households. Among Spanish-origin households, poverty has increased for all family types, and there has been a significant growth in female-headed households. The increase in poverty has been caused by a rise in the number of families, rather than increases in the rate of poverty. The rate of poverty has remained high but steady, while the number of Spanish-origin families has grown. In 1972 the poverty rate for two-parent and male-headed families was 17.4 percent; in 1984 it was 17.1 percent. There were 1.5 million poor in such families in 1972 and 2.7 million in 1984. The poverty rate for female-headed households did not change markedly (53.5 percent in 1972; 53.4 percent in 1984), but the number of these households increased significantly. In 1974 there were 462,000 female-headed households (see Table 2.4); by 1984 the number had risen by 95 percent to 905,000. The 211,000 poor Spanish-origin families headed by a woman in 1972 expanded to 483,000 by 1984, an increase of 128 percent (see Table 2.1). Thus, Spanish-origin households of all types have suffered increases in poverty. The number of female-headed households has increased significantly, and their rate of poverty is even higher than for other Spanish-origin households.

Summary: The Causes of the
Feminization of Poverty, by Race

The feminization of poverty has in considerable measure resulted from large increases in the number of female household
heads, and a high and basically steady rate of poverty for such
families. Decreases in the poverty rate of black two-parent
families have also contributed to the predominance of families
headed by women among the black poverty population. Currently almost half of all the poor in America live in households
headed by single women. A majority of all poor children in
America live in female-headed families, with almost 75 percent of all poor black children living in families headed by
single women.

The Impact of Women's Poverty
on Children

Poverty among children is on the increase. There were more
poor children in 1982, 1983, and 1984 (about 13 million) than
in any year since 1965 (see Table 2.5). The number of poor
children increased by about 3 million in the short period between 1979 and 1984. This was true despite the fact that the
total population of children decreased by 9 million between
1968 and 1983. In 1982, 1983, and 1984, over 21 percent of all
the nation's children were poor. This was the highest rate of
poverty among children since the early 1960s.

Breaking the figures down by race yields some interesting
insights. As Table 2.5 shows, the majority of all poor children
are white. In 1984, 62 percent of all poor children were white,
only slightly above the percentage throughout the 1960s and
1970s. The poverty rate for white children in 1982, 1983, and

1984 was 16 percent. This was the highest rate of poverty for white children since the early 1960s and a significant increase over the 1970s, when the rate averaged 11 percent.

Poverty among black children has also been increasing. In 1984 there were 4.3 million poor black children. This was slightly below the 4.4 million black children who were poor in 1982, but higher than most years during the 1970s. The rate of poverty for black children in 1984 was 46.2 percent, an increase over the rates that prevailed during the 1970s, when an average of 41 percent of all black children were poor. The rate of poverty for black children is almost triple the rate for white children.

Figures for Spanish-origin children have only been available since 1973, but they indicate that poverty among children in these families has also been increasing. The poverty rate for Spanish-origin children increased from 27.8 percent in 1973 to 38.7 percent in 1984.

The data in Table 2.6 strongly suggest that the increase in female-headed families has played a major role in the increase in poverty among children. Over half of all poor children in America now live in female-headed households, compared to less than 25 percent in the late 1950s and early 1960s. By the 1970s an average of 53 percent of all the poor children in America lived in families headed by single women, with a high of 58.5 percent in 1978. The average for 1980-84 was 51.6 percent. The poverty rate for children in female-headed households (Bureau of the Census 1985, 21) has remained over 50 percent in every year since 1959 except one (in 1979 it was 48.6 percent).

As noted in Chapter 1, a congressional study reported in 1985 that a statistical simulation it conducted estimated that the number of poor children in 1983 might have been almost 3 million, or 22 percent lower, had the proportion of children living in female-headed families not increased (Ways and Means 1985, 7). Chapter 3 provides further empirical evidence

Table 2.5 **Number of Children Below the Poverty Level by Race of Family Head**

	All*	Poverty rate	White family head	Percent of all poor children†	Poverty rate	Black family head	Percent of all poor children*	Poverty rate	Spanish-origin family head	Percent of all poor children	Poverty rate
1984	12,929	21.0	8,086	62.5	16.1	4,320	33.4	46.2	2,317	17.9	38.7
1983	13,449	21.8	8,556	63.0	17.0	4,273	31.0	46.2	2,251	16.1	37.7
1982	13,139	21.3	8,282	63.0	16.5	4,388	33.9	47.3	2,117	16.1	38.9
1981	12,068	19.5	7,429	61.5	14.7	4,170	34.5	44.9	1,874	15.3	35.4
1980	11,114	17.9	6,817	61.3	13.4	3,906	35.1	42.1	1,718	15.4	33.0
1979	9,993	16.0	5,909	59.1	11.4	3,745	37.5	40.8	1,505	15.0	27.7
1978	9,722	15.7	5,674	58.4	11.0	3,781	38.9	41.2	1,354	13.9	27.2
1977	10,028	16.0	5,943	59.3	11.4	3,850	38.4	41.6	1,402	14.0	28.0
1976	10,081	15.8	6,034	59.8	11.3	3,758	37.3	40.4	1,424	14.1	30.1
1975	10,882	16.8	6,748	62.0	12.5	3,884	35.7	41.4	1,619	14.8	33.1
1974	9,967	15.1	6,079	60.9	11.0	3,713	37.2	39.6	1,414	14.2	28.6
1973	9,453	14.2	5,462	57.8	9.7	3,822	40.4	40.6	1,364	14.4	27.8
1972	10,082	14.9	5,784	57.4	10.1	4,025	39.9	42.7			
1971	10,344	15.1	6,341	61.3	10.9	3,836	37.1	40.7			
1970	10,235	14.9	6,138	60.0	10.5	3,922	38.3	41.5			
1969	9,501	13.8	5,667	59.6	9.7	3,677	38.7	39.6			
1968	10,739	15.3	6,373	59.3	10.7	4,188	38.9	43.1			
1967	11,427	16.3	6,729	58.8	11.3	4,558	39.9	47.4			
1966	12,146	17.4	7,204	59.3	12.1	4,774	39.3	50.6			
1965	14,388	20.7	8,595	59.7	14.4	5,022	35.0	65.5			
1960	17,288	26.5	11,299	64.9	20.0						
1959	17,208	26.9	11,386	66.1	20.6						

*Includes all related children under 18.

†Percentages do not add up to 100 because children of Spanish origin can be of any race.

Source: Bureau of the Census (1985). "Money Income and Poverty Status of Families and Persons in the United States: 1984," *Current Population Reports*, series P-60, no. 149, p. 21.

that the growth in female-headed families is directly related to increaing poverty among American children.

Poor White Children

The data in Table 2.6 show the severity of poverty for children in both white and minority female-headed families. Between 1959 and 1984 the number of poor white children in female-headed families increased by 39 percent from 2.4 million to 3.4 million. The rate of poverty for children in these families averaged 41.9 percent during the 1970s, reaching 45.9 percent in 1984. During the 1970s more than 40 percent of all poor white children lived in female-headed families. Because of significant increases during the early 1980s in rates of poverty for white male-headed families, the percentage dropped to 39.2 percent in 1982 and 39.7 percent in 1983, and then rose to 41 percent in 1984.

Poor Black Children

Poverty among children in black female-headed families is considerably worse, with the number of such children rising by 119 percent—from 1.5 million in 1959 to 3.2 million in 1984. The percentage of all poor black children who live in female-headed families increased steadily from the late 1950s, stabilizing in the mid- to high 70s in recent years. In 1984 almost one out of every two black children in America lived in poverty, and 74 percent of these children lived in female-headed families. The poverty rate for children in black female-headed families averaged 66.7 percent between 1970 and 1984. In 1984 the poverty rate was still 66.2 percent. These figures are particularly ominous since the data indicate that three out of four black children can expect to spend some of their childhood in a single-parent family (Bumpass and Rindfuss 1979, 53). The overwhelming majority of all black single-parent families are female-headed.

Table 2.6

Poor Children in Female-headed Families (No Husband Present)

	Number	Percent of all poor children*	Poverty rate	Number of white poor children	Percent of white poor children*	Poverty rate
1984	6,772	52.0	54.0	3,377	41.0	45.9
1983	6,758	51.0	55.5	3,399	39.0	47.2
1982	6,696	51.0	56.0	3,249	39.2	46.5
1981	6,305	52.2	52.3	3,120	42.0	47.8
1980	5,866	52.8	50.8	2,813	41.3	41.6
1979	5,635	56.4	48.6	2,629	44.5	38.6
1978	5,687	58.5	50.6	2,627	46.3	39.9
1977	5,658	56.4	50.3	2,693	45.3	40.3
1976	5,583	55.4	52.0	2,713	45.0	42.7
1975	5,597	51.4	52.7	2,813	41.7	44.2
1974	5,361	53.8	51.5	2,683	44.1	42.9
1973	5,171	54.7	52.1	2,461	45.0	42.1
1972	5,094	50.5	52.2	2,273	39.3	41.1
1971	4,850	46.9	53.1	2,452	38.6	44.6
1970	4,689	45.8	53.0	2,247	36.6	43.1
1969	4,247	44.7	54.4	2,068	36.5	45.2
1968	4,409	41.0	55.2	2,075	32.5	44.4
1967	4,246	37.1	54.3	1,930	28.7	42.1
1966	4,262	35.0	58.2	2,112	29.3	46.9
1965	4,562	31.7	64.2	2,321	26.9	52.9
1960	4,095	23.7	68.4	2,357	21.0	59.9
1959	4,145	24.1	72.2	2,420	21.2	64.6
Percentage		63.0			39.0	

Source: Bureau of the Census (1985) "Money Income and Poverty Status of Families and Persons in the United States: 1984" (Advance Data from the March 1985 Current Population Survey), *Current Population Reports*, series P-60, no. 149, pp. 21–23.

Poor Spanish-Origin Children

The data for Spanish-origin children reveal a slightly different picture. While the number of poor children in female-headed families has increased significantly, their percentage of the

	Number of black poor children	Percent of black poor children	Poverty rate	Number of Spanish-origin poor children	Percent of Spanish-origin poor children	Poverty rate
1984	3,234	74.8	66.	1,093	47.2	71.0
1983	3,187	74.6	68.3	1,018	45.2	70.6
1982	3,269	74.5	70.7	990	46.8	71.8
1981	3,051	73.2	67.7	909	48.5	67.3
1980	2,944	75.4	64.8	809	47.1	65.0
1979	2,887	77.1	63.1	668	44.4	62.2
1978	2,948	78.0	66.4	663	44.0	68.9
1977	2,885	74.9	65.7	686	48.9	68.6
1976	2,778	73.9	65.6	636	44.7	67.3
1975	2,724	70.1	66.0	694	42.9	68.4
1974	2,651	71.4	65.0	621	43.9	64.3
1973	2,635	68.9	67.2	606	44.4	68.7
1972	2,686	66.7	69.5			
1971	2,329	60.7	66.6			
1970	2,383	60.7	67.7			
1969	2,137	58.1	68.2			
1968	2,241	54.1	70.5			
1967	2,265	49.1	72.4			
1966	2,107	44.1	76.6			
1959	1,475	29.4	81.6			

Spanish-origin poor has not. This indicates that poverty has risen significantly for both male- and female-headed Spanish-origin families. Between 1973 and 1984 an average of 45.6 percent of all poor Spanish-origin children lived in female-headed households, with only modest yearly variation. The

Figure 2.1   **Poverty Rates for Children,* 1984**

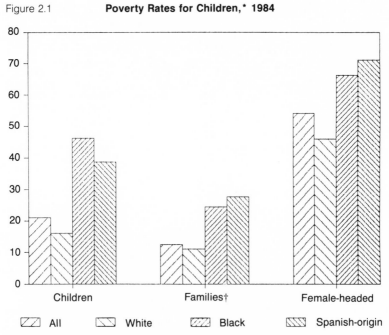

Source: Bureau of the Census (1985) ''Money Income and Poverty Status of Families and Persons in the United States: 1984,'' *Current Population Reports*, series P-60, no. 149, pp. 20-23.

*Related children under 18.

†Includes both married-couple families and male-headed families with no wife present.

poverty rate for children in these female-headed families, however, is extremely high. During 1982, 1983, and 1984 over 70 percent of all children in families headed by women lived in poverty.

Figure 2.1 graphically reveals how strikingly at variance rates of poverty are for children of different races and in various types of families. Children in general suffer high rates of poverty when compared to other groups in our society, but those in intact families have much lower rates of poverty than do those in families headed by a single woman. All children, regardless of race, suffer extremely high rates of poverty when

Table 2.7

Poverty Rates per 100 Children by Family Type and Race, 1983

Children	Black	White	Spanish orign	All children under 18 years
Total	46.7	17.3	38.2	22.2
In female-headed families (total)	68.5	47.6	70.5	55.8
Mothers:				
Never married	77.2	71.3	85.8	75.1
Separated or divorced	66.8	47.3	70.1	53.5
Widowed	60.7	27.9	38.9	41.1
In male-present families	23.8	11.9	27.3	13.5

Source: Committee on Ways and Means (1985) *Children in Poverty*, House of Representatives, 99th Congress (Washington, D.C.: U.S. Government Printing Office).

they live only with their mother. The poverty rates for Spanish-origin and black children in female-headed families are particularly striking.

Table 2.7 breaks down the poverty rates for children according to whether the female head of a family has ever been married, and, if so, how the marriage ended. The highest rates of poverty are suffered by children of women who have never been married. Over 70 percent of all the children in such families are poor, reaching almost 86 percent for Spanish-origin children. Children of widows, especially white and Spanish-origin children, suffer the lowest rates of poverty.

Conclusions

The data presented show the changes in poverty demographics that have resulted in women and their dependent children becoming an increasingly large proportion of all the official poor in America. Currently almost half of all the poor in America live in female-headed households. More than half of all the poor children in America live in homes headed by single women, including over 70 percent of all poor black children.

The rate of poverty for female-headed households has always been high, and it has not changed dramatically over the last fifteen years (see the caveats in footnote 1). What has changed is the number of female-headed households. As this type of household has increased, the high rate of poverty borne by this type of family unit has greatly increased the number of poor women and children. Chapter 3 presents a statistical analysis that lends weight to these conclusions.

Female-Headed Households: Growth and Poverty

This chapter first seeks to explain why an increasingly large proportion of American households are headed by women. Then, the professional literature is reviewed to provide insights into why a disproportionate percentage of all female-headed households are poor. Finally, an empirical analysis is carried out to isolate statistically the antecedents of poverty among female-headed households.

The Increase in Female Heads of Household

One of the obvious questions raised by the analysis in Chapter 2 is, why has the number of female household heads increased so drastically? There is a considerable literature on this topic (Cooney 1979; Cutright 1974; Korbin 1973; Lantz, Martin, and O'Hara 1977; Ross and Sawhill 1975). In addition to population growth, research indicates that the change has resulted from an aging population with more widows, greatly increased rates of divorce and separation, later marriages and less remarriage, and higher rates of out-of-wedlock births. Differing methodologies give each of these factors a somewhat different weight, but all conclude that women are now much more likely than they were in the past to form independent households (Ways and Means 1985, 66).

Mortality and Marriage Rates

Among older women the increase in household heads in part reflects the differences in male and female mortality. Life expectancy of women at 65 exceeds that of men by 4.5 years (National Center for Health Statistics 1982, table 3). Older women who become single increasingly elect to maintain their own households rather than live with others. Widowed women are less likely than widowed men to remarry (Bureau of the Census 1976, table C). By 1980 more than half of all women over 65 were maintaining separate residences.

For younger women the increase in household heads is the product of later marriages, a higher divorce and separation rate, an increase in single parenting, and less hesitation about living away from parents. Younger women are now on average marrying some two years later than they did in the 1950s (Cherlin 1980). In 1950 the average age of first marriage was 20.3; in 1980 it was 22.1. In 1950 only about one-fourth of all 20–24-year-old women had never been married. By 1980 the proportion had risen to 45 percent (Bureau of the Census 1982b, table 1).

Table 3.1

Divorce and Separation Rates, 1960–1982

Sex	Year	White	Black		Sex	Year	White	Black
M	1960	27	45		F	1960	38	78
M	1970	32	62		F	1970	56	104
M	1975	51	96		F	1975	77	178
M	1979	66	152		F	1979	102	243
M	1980	74	151		F	1980	110	257
M	1982	86	176		F	1982	128	265

Source: Bureau of the Census (1985) *Statistical Abstract of the United States 1984*. 104th ed., U.S. Department of Commerce, table 55, p. 45.

Divorce and Separation

Divorce and separation have increased dramatically over the same period (Bane 1976; Cherlin 1981; Clayton and Voss 1977; Glick and Spanier 1980; Lasch 1980; Moore and Waite 1981). The number of divorced persons per 1,000 active marriages increased from 35 in 1960 to 114 in 1982. The rate for women and minorities is even higher (see Table 3.1).

The data, perhaps deceptive since they do not control income level and age of first marriage, nonetheless suggest that black women have a much higher rate of divorce than any other group. In simple numerical terms, the rate of divorce for black women is more than twice the rate for white women. Black women are also much more likely to be separated from their husband, and separations have been increasing. In 1960, 12.4 percent of all black women and 1.7 percent of all white women reported being separated (Bureau of the Census 1981, p. 39). By 1982, the figures were 17.3 percent and 3.5 percent, respectively.

Divorce and separation, then, have increased greatly since the 1960s, especially for black women. The early 1970s were the first years in American history when more marriages ended in divorce than in death. Cherlin (1981, 23) estimates that almost one-half of the marriages that took place in the 1970s will end in divorce. When divorce occurs, remarriage is now less likely. The remarriage rate for women age 25 to 44 declined 30 percent between 1970 and 1980.

Out-of-Wedlock Births

Another factor that has significantly increased the number of female-headed families is out-of-wedlock births (Furstenberg 1976; Furstenberg, Lincoln, and Menken 1981; Hofferth and Moore 1979; Moore and Burt 1981; Moore and Caldwell 1976; Scharf 1979; Vinovskis 1981). Since 1950 such births have more than quadrupled, rising from 142,000 in 1950 to 666,000 in 1980 (SCCYF 1983, 4). The raw data show that unmarried black women have children at a much higher rate than do unmarried white women. In 1979 there were 316,000 children born to unmarried black women, compared to 263,000 born to unwed white women. White women, of course, greatly outnumber black women in the U.S. population. Of all women age 15 and over in 1981, 89 percent were white (Bureau of the Census 1982b, 14).

Research by Pittman (SCCYF 1983, 122) shows that "black teenagers are 1.5 times more likely to get pregnant, 3.5 times more likely to give birth and 5.5 times more likely to be unmarried parents." Still, race may not be an independent predictor. Young women from low-income families—regardless of race—are much more likely to become pregnant while still teenagers. White teenagers who become pregnant are more likely than black teenagers to obtain an abortion or marry before the birth of the child (Furstenberg, Lincoln, and Menken 1981, 27-31).

While births to unmarried women have increased, births to married women have declined. The result is that a growing proportion of all children are born out of wedlock. In 1950, 4 percent of all children were born to unwed mothers; by 1980, the figure was 18.4 percent. The increase is far greater for black women. In 1980, 55.3 percent of all black children born in America had an unmarried mother, whereas only 11 percent of all white children had an unwed mother (SCCYF 1983, 4).

In many cases these figures represent striking changes in a relatively short period of time. As recently as the early 1960s, 75 percent of all black families were headed by a married couple. By 1984 this was true of only 51 percent of all black families. The contrast with white and Spanish-origin families is stark. In 1984, 72 percent of all Spanish-origin families and 84 percent of all white families were headed by a married couple (Bureau of the Census 1985a, 6–8). In 1960 about 70 percent of all black children under age 3 lived with both parents. By 1982 only 40 percent lived with both parents. About 85 percent of all white children under age 3 lived with both parents in 1982.

The percentage of all single-parent families headed by a woman who has never been married has also increased significantly. In 1970 only 1 percent of single mothers had never been married. The figure in 1984 was 6.3 percent. Among black women the percentage increased from 5 percent in 1970 to 28 percent. Among whites it grew ninefold, to 2.7 percent.

There is a growing literature that concludes that single parenting and divorce and separation rates correlate significantly with demographic and economic variables (Guttentag and Secord 1983, 199–230). When the number of available women significantly outnumbers available men, illegitimacy and marital disruption increase. This is a particularly significant problem for the black population. In the United States in general, and more acutely in some major urban areas, young black women greatly outnumber young black men (Guttentag and Secord 1983, 214; Jackson 1973, 23). Infant mortality rates, teenage mortality rates, and military service seem to contribute to the imbalanced sex ratios. Poor men, regardless of race, are also less likely to marry and support a family. Young black men suffer particularly high unemployment rates and are thus less able to support a family.

The factors reviewed here seem to be the major contributors to the growth of female households. But why do female householders suffer such a high rate of poverty?

Antecedents of Female-Household Poverty

Studies have isolated many of the factors that combine to produce high rates of poverty among female households. This section discusses some of the major variables and assesses their predictive insights.

Lack of Adequate Child Support

One of the most obvious factors contributing to the poverty of female-headed families is the low level of child support by absent fathers (Bureau of the Census 1980). In recent years on average only some 35 percent of all women with minor children from an absent father have received child support, and of these only about 68 percent have received the agreed upon amount (SCCYF 1983, 20). Figures for 1978 provide examples from a typical year. In 1978 there were 7.1 million women with children from an absent father. Sixty-eight percent of these women were awarded child support but only 35 percent actually received support payments. These payments averaged $1,799 annually. Support was low even when the number of children in the family was large. The annual average for women with four or more children receiving support was $2,752. By 1981 the average payment to all families had risen to $2,110, but in real dollars this represented a decline in purchasing power of about 16 percent (SCCYF 1983, 37). Thus, most mothers did not receive any support, and those who did

Table 3.2

Child Support, by Race

Race	Number of women (in millions)	Percent awarded support	Percent receiving support	Mean annual support
White	5.1	71%	43%	$1,861
Black	1.9	29%	14%	$1,294
Spanish	0.5	44%	24%	$1,318

Source: Select Committee on Children, Youth, and Families (1983) "U.S. Children and Their Families: 1983," 98th Congress, 1st Session (Washington, D.C.: GPO), p. 20.

tended to receive only modest amounts.

White women generally receive more support than do minority women. The data in Table 3.2 (which do not control for the socioeconomic status of the father) suggest considerable variance in support by race. None of the family types received decent levels of financial support, but white women were more often awarded support and were more likely to receive the support awarded. Only 29 percent of black women were awarded support, and only 14 percent actually received any payments. The situation was little better for women of Spanish origin. Given these data, it is not surprising that studies show that men tend to be better off financially after a divorce, whereas women tend to end up in a worse financial condition (Espenshade 1979; Weitzman 1980).

Ironically, perhaps, women below the poverty level are more likely than any other group to receive support from an absent ex-husband. Because of federal and state laws (see Chapter 4), about 60 percent of all women below the poverty level with minor children receive some support. This is much higher than the rates for middle-income women, suggesting that the problem is not entirely financial. There is, however, clearly a financial antecedent. A number of studies have shown that low-income black males have conventional attitudes toward marriage and family life, but high rates of unemployment and limited income make it difficult for them to be stable providers and marriage partners (Levy 1980, 42–46; Ross and Sawill 1975, 74, 86). Young black men have higher rates of unemployment than any other group. In 1982, 20.1 percent of all black males over age 16 were unemployed. Among 16- to 19-year-olds the rate was 48.9 percent, and for 20- to 24-year-olds it was 31.5 percent.

Fertility Rates

Fertility rates also seem to contribute to poverty. The more children a woman has to support, the more likely the family is to be poor (Bureau of the Census 1985a, 29). In 1984, for example, 33.3 percent of all female household heads with one child were poor, rising to 66 percent of those with three children, and 79 percent of those with four children. The poverty rates for minority women were even higher. Fifty-seven percent of all black female family heads with two children lived in poverty.

Minority women have the highest fertility rates, but the differences between the races have narrowed as fertility rates have dropped for all women. The 1950 fertility rate of 106 children per 1,000 women, for example had dropped to 71 by 1981. As late as 1970 the difference between the races was major: white women had a fertility rate of 84, compared to 115 for black women. In 1981 the rate for white women was 68, compared to 81 for black women.

Fertility rates also seem to contribute to poverty in several other ways. First, the younger women are when they have children, the more children they are likely to have. The more children a woman has, the less likely she is to be able to support them. Additionally, about 80 percent of teenage mothers never complete high school. Thus, teenage mothers suffer earning handicaps that generally last a lifetime. Minority women tend both to have children earlier and to have more children (Bureau of the Census 1985a, 29). Women with two or more children have lower rates of employment, lower employment and career aspirations, and lower wage earnings (Carlson and Stinson 1982; Cramer 1980; Smith-Loving and Tickamyer 1978; Smith-Loving and Tickamyer 1982).

Employment and Wages

The economic condition of female household heads is also affected by a series of problems related to employment and wage earnings (Chafetz 1984, 47–79). Most obviously, unemployment rates for poor female family heads are very high (Bureau of the Census 1985a, 29). In 1984, 66.3 percent of all such women were unemployed. The rate was very high for white women (56.4 percent), but even higher for blacks (77.6 percent).

Studies conducted at the Institute for Research on Poverty demonstrated how significantly unemployment rates impact on poor families. The studies revealed that a 10 percent increase in the unemployment rate is associated with about a 2.5 percent increase in the incidence of pretransfer (before government transfers) poverty. Thus, if unemployment increased from 9 to 10 percent, the number of families with earnings below the poverty level would increase from 20 percent to 20.5 percent, adding over a million new people to the ranks of the poor (SCCYF 1984, 63).

Even when female family heads are employed they tend to earn less than male heads of households (Beller 1980; Beller 1982; Burstein 1979; Kessler-Harris 1982; King 1978; Polachek 1979; Rytina 1982; Trieman and Hartmann 1981; U.S. Commission on Civil Rights 1982). In 1984 female family heads had a median income from all sources (i.e., wages, welfare benefits, and child support) of $12,803, compared to $29,612 for married couple families (Bureau of the Census

1985a, 6). Minority female family heads had significantly lower median incomes—$8,648 for black heads and $8,452 for Spanish-origin heads.

Women workers in general earn significantly less than male workers, for a number of reasons. Many more women work only part time or part of the year. Women also tend to change jobs and move in and out of the work force more frequently. However, even when women work full time year-round, they earn much less than similarly employed men. In 1984, for example, such women had median earnings of $15,422, compared to $24,004 for their male counterparts (Bureau of the Census 1985, 13–4). The discrepancy is caused by many factors. First, the mean age of working women is considerably younger than that of male employees (which means that women tend to have less seniority). Second, women employees tend to be concentrated in jobs traditionally considered "women's work," and these jobs usually pay a rather low wage regardless of the skill and training required. Third, there is solid empirical evidence of pay discrimination as recently as the 1970s, and some discrimination may continue (see Cocoran and Duncan 1979; Bergman 1974; Lloyd and Niemi 1979; Suter and Miller 1973; Wolf and Fligstein 1979).

The economic condition of all families has also been affected over the last twenty years by inflation. Increases in median family earnings have not been large enough to keep up with inflation. In 1970, for example, the median income for all families was $25,317. In constant dollar terms it was only $26,438 in 1984 (Bureau of the Census 1985a, 10). All racial groups have suffered declines in real purchasing power. A recent congressional study found that the poorest 20 percent of all families have suffered the worst declines in purchasing power. In 1968 such families received 7.4 percent of all income; by 1983, they received only 4.8 percent (Ways and Means 1985, 167).

Welfare Benefits

The combination of unemployment, low wages, and little or no child support leaves millions of female household heads in financial distress. Cash welfare benefits (and Social Security benefits for those who qualify) are generally too modest to alleviate the problem. In June 1984, for example, the average monthly AFDC payment to families was $316.84, or $108.74 per recipient (Duvall, Gondreau, and Marsh 1982, 5; Social Security Administration 1985, 11). Many states provided benefits considerably below these averages (see Chapter 4). The result is that the vast majority of female-headed families with no income other than AFDC live below the poverty line (Social Security Administration 1982, 1). There is also evidence that AFDC rules prompt some families to break up and encourage some women to delay marriage or remarriage (Bahr 1979; Hannan, Tuma, and Groenveld 1977; Moles 1979). The Reagan administration has cut back on welfare benefits, further increasing the income deficits of female-headed families (see Chapter 4).

The Income Deficit

The cumulative result of all the financial calamities that befall poor female-headed families is the rapid increase in their income deficit (see Table 3.3). In 1984 the income of the average poor female-headed family was $4,331 below the poverty level for the family size. This was a very substantial increase from 1978, when the deficit averaged $2,483: The deficit is even larger for minority families. Further, the increase has been most notable under the Reagan administration. The deficit declined or was fairly stable until 1979 but has increased rapidly since then.

Table 3.3

Poor Female-Headed Families: Mean Income Deficit

	All	White	Black	Spanish-origin
1984	4,331	4,027	4,691	4,764
1983	4,269	3,980	4,645	4,581
1982	4,076	3,806	4,219	4,312
1981	3,694	3,289	4,219	3,739
1980	3,216	2,922	3,582	3,248
1979	2,843	2,697	3,008	2,732
1978	2,483	2,251	2,720	2,334
1977	2,239	2,088	2,415	1,962
1976	2,029	1,896	2,180	1,779
1975	2,052	1,890	2,296	
1974	2,097	1,972	2,270	
1973	2,041	1,955	2,136	
1972	2,079	1,930	2,237	
1971	2,138	2,117	2,168	
1970	2,223	2,043	2,451	
1969	2,149	1,979	2,399	
1968	2,338	2,238	2,445	
1967	2,277	2,111	2,511	
1963	2,731	2,527		
1959	2,599	2,447		

Source: Bureau of the Census, "Money Income and Poverty Status of Families and Persons in the United States," *Current Population Reports*, series P-60, various years.

Summary

This review yields numerous insights into factors associated with high rates of poverty among female-headed households. High rates of unemployment, low wages and income (from all sources), inadequate child support, increased rates of divorce and separation, increases in out-of-wedlock births, and differences in rates of fertility all seem to contribute to poverty. In the section that follows, correlational analysis is used to measure the association between these variables and changes in the number of poor in female-headed households.

Statistical Correlates of Poverty in Female-Headed Households: By Race

The Dependent Variable

The analysis reported in Table 3.4 uses number of poor in female-headed households by year as the dependent variable. These data are reported in Table 2.2. The analysis was run for all poor female-headed households, and then separately for white and black households. The analysis for Spanish-origin households is not reported because data for such households are often incomplete, and preliminary analysis revealed that there are major differences among the groups that compose the Spanish-origin population (Burke, Gabe, Rimkunas, and Griffith 1985, 29). The Cuban population, for example, is quite different from the Puerto Rican population. Thus, the composite image yielded by group analysis is not very useful.

The analysis also had to be limited to the years in which reliable data for all the independent variables could be obtained, and this varied by racial group. The analysis for all poor female-headed families covers the period 1960–1983. For white families the analysis covers 1966 to 1983, and for black families 1972 to 1983.

The Independent Variables

Table 3.2 shows the simple correlations (Pearson's R's) between the annual number of poor in female-headed households and nine independent variables. The first independent variable is rate of unemployment for female family heads. This variable includes family heads who report themselves to be either unemployed or out of the labor market. The second, third, and fourth variables are designed to measure the income deficiencies of female family heads. The first measure used is the annual size of the income deficit (mean dollars below the poverty level for family size) suffered by poor female-headed families. The second (Gap1) is the yearly dollar difference between the median income of two-parent families (the wife may or may not be employed) and female-headed families. The third income variable (Gap2) is the yearly dollar difference between the median income of male and female workers. The information needed to construct these variables is reported yearly in the P-60 series of *Current Population Reports*.

The fifth variable is annual rate of divorce. Of several possible measures of divorce, the one used here is divorces per 1,000 married women age 15 and over. The sixth variable is annual number of out-of-wedlock births. The seventh variable is yearly fertility rate. The measure is the number of births per 1,000 women. The data used to generate variables six, seven, and eight are collected by the U.S. National Center for Health Statistics and reported annually or semi-annually in *Vital Statistics*. The eighth variable is the annual percentage of all families headed by a single woman. The last variable is the unemployment rate for males age 16 and over.

Findings: By Race

The measures of association reported in table 3.4 lend support to most of the explanations of female-household poverty discussed above. All three of the income measures correlate significantly with number of poor in female-headed households. Since aggregate data usually generate high associations, the differences in the magnitudes of the R's are probably not large enough to yield reliable information about which of the measures of income deficiency is the most insightful. What the associations do suggest, however, is that low wages and income (from all sources) and inadequate child support contribute significantly to the problem of poverty among female-headed families.

Number of out-of-wedlock births correlates strongly, but, as expected, the separate analysis by race shows that this is a

Table 3.4

Correlates of Female-Family Poverty: By Race*

	Poor in female-headed families	Poor in white F-H families	Poor in black F-H families
1. Rate of unemployment	.26†	.73	.44†
2. Income deficit	.74	.86	.72
3. Income gap1	.96	.86	.97
4. Income gap2	.91	.83	.73
5. Rate of divorce	.88	.64	.92
6. Out-of-wedlock births	.90	.53†	.94
7. Fertility rate	.24†	.08†	.82
8. Percent of families F-H	.74	.61†	.91
9. Rate of unemployment (men)	.70	.12†	.66

*Pearson's R's.
†Not statistically significant. All the other correlations are significant at .001 or above level of confidence.

significant predictor only for black families. Similarly, fertility rate is a significant correlate only for black families.

Unemployment shows a reverse relationship. It is significant only for white households. For blacks this variable correlates insignificantly because there is much less variance over the years. Rate of divorce is also associated with increasing poverty. As the raw data suggest, divorce is a somewhat more important factor for black than for white women. Increases in the percentage of all households headed by women also correlate with increases in poverty, but this is again a stronger correlate for black households.

One of the most interesting variables is the rate of unemployment for males age 16 and over. Notice that this variable is a significant correlate for all female-headed households, but the racial breakdown shows that it is really important only for black households. This finding seems reasonable since unemployment is so much higher for young black males than for any other group and would seem to make many of them incapable of supporting a family. These high rates of unemployment also seem logically related to the increases in single parenting, and to the high rates of divorce and separation, which we have shown to be related to persisting, even growing, poverty within the black population.

The differences in the levels of association for each racial group suggest that income deficiencies, high levels of unemployment, and increasing rates of divorce are the best predictors of poverty for white families. For black families, out-of-wedlock births, high rates of divorce, income deficiencies, and high rates of unemployment for young men seem particularly important.[1]

Conclusions

A number of factors have contributed to the increase in female-headed households, most importantly the increasing rates of divorce, separation, and single parenting. Regardless of race, female-headed households tend to have low incomes (especially compared to male and two-parent families) and high rates of unemployment. Welfare benefits do not come close to compensating for the income deficiencies of poor female-headed families, and under the Reagan administration benefits have been

1. Numerous attempts were made to use multiple regression analysis to estimate the collective predictive power of the independent variables. None of these attempts was successful. Separate runs were made for each of the three major groups (all, white, black). Because the income deficiency variables are obviously intercorrelated, a separate run using each of the four income variables (along with the other independent variables) was made for each of the three major groups. This technique limited but did not eliminate serious problems of multicollinearity. The intercorrelations between the remaining independent variables were generally quite high, and too pervasive to be eliminated by selecting variables for exclusion. The Durbin-Watts test did not reveal serial correlation. The R squares produced by the regression analysis were over .90 for each of the three groups regardless of the income deficiency variable used but the standardized betas were erratic and the standard errors quite large.

steadily reduced. Some other types of social welfare programs, such as family planning services, also seem to fail to reach the clients who need them most.

There are somewhat different correlates of poverty in black and white female-headed households. Black female-headed households often become the victims of poverty because of high rates of divorce, out-of-wedlock births, and fertility, combined with limited sources of income from employment, child support, and social welfare programs. The staggering rate of unemployment suffered by black males correlates strongly with rates of poverty among black female-headed households. A causal relationship between the rates of unemployment among black men and the high rates of divorce, abandonment, and out-of-wedlock births that seem to cause much of the poverty in the black population seems apparent, but it needs to be more rigorously tested.

White female-headed households seem to fall into poverty because of increasing rates of divorce, high rates of unemployment, and limited sources of income, including inadequate social welfare services and child support.

Two major problems, then, lie at the heart of increased rates of poverty among women. The first is the nation's continuing high rates of unemployment and subemployment for both men and women. Second is the nation's failure to adapt and expand its social policy to the changing role of women.

Chapter 4

Female-Headed Families: The Social Welfare Response

Of all the major Western industrial nations, the United States has always been the laggard in social welfare policy. America's welfare programs are the most recent in origin and the most limited in design, coverage, and cost (OECD 1976, 17; Wilensky 1975, 11). And despite their modesty, American welfare programs rest on very tentative and reluctant public support (see Feagin 1975).

The Positive State

In a recent article Furniss and Mitchell (1984) analyzed how social welfare provisions differ among Western industrial nations, and related these differences to the public philosophies that guide the economic and political systems of each nation. Their analysis revealed that each of the major Western nations has a complex public philosophy that defines—and sets limits on—the role of the state in the economic and political systems. To isolate the similarities and differences among nations, Furniss and Mitchell offered a framework for analyzing social welfare systems based on three major criteria: the design and goals of the programs; the political, economic, and social priorities reflected by them; and the impact of the programs on recipients and the political and economic systems. This analytical framework produced four state types: the Positive state, the Social Security state, the Democratic Corporatist state, and the Social Welfare state.

Furniss and Mitchell argue that the American system approximates the Positive state—the least developed form. In the Positive state, welfare policy is primarily a means of social control based on "free market" principles. Social welfare programs are designed to protect holders of property from the difficulties of unregulated markets and from demands for redistribution of income. The authors agree with Wilensky (1975, 109) that the poor in America are given just enough to "defang the revolutionary tiger." The resistance of the American philosophy to social welfare programs is so ingrained, in fact, that only acute crisis has prompted the establishment and most of the expansion of such programs (Leman 1977).

The Historical Context

Decades after the other major Western industrial nations had begun developing welfare programs, the United States established its first, very limited and modest programs in response to the economic collapse of the Great Depression, which began in 1929 (Piven and Cloward 1971; 1979). The collapse was so massive that by 1933 one-fourth of the nation's adult men were unemployed, millions of families were losing their homes, and thousands stood in breadlines each day. Millions of those who suffered from the economic crisis were former middle-class citizens, registered voters, who became more and more willing to support radical remedies (Rodgers 1979, 43–72). Still, the government's response was slow. Between 1933 and 1935, President Franklin D. Roosevelt centered his attention on emergency measures such as public works projects and prevention of bank closures.

By 1935 the crisis had deepened. The Works Project Administration (WPA) had provided jobs for millions of U.S. citizens, but some 8 million males were still unemployed. It has been estimated that WPA provided jobs to only one of every four applicants (Piven and Cloward 1971, 98). Those millions who could not find work, along with the aged, handicapped, and orphans, turned to state and local governments for assistance. Many states, however, could not handle the burden. Some cut the size of grants so that more of the needy could receive some assistance; others abolished all assistance. New Jersey offered the indigent licenses to beg (Piven and Cloward 1971, 109).

The Social Security Act of 1935

The continuing hardship spawned more and more radical criticism of the Roosevelt administration. Under these pressures, the president launched what historians refer to as the "second New Deal." This New Deal had two primary thrusts. First, the government would use Keynesian economics (to stimulate and, it was hoped, regulate economic cycles) and increased assistance to business to promote an economic recovery. Second, the government would establish, through the Social Security Act of 1935, assistance programs for those who were outside the labor force.

The Social Security Act consisted of five major titles.

- Title I provided grants to the states for assistance to the aged;
- Title II established the social security system;
- Title III provided grants to the states for the administration of unemployment compensation;
- Title IV established the Aid to Dependent Children (ADC) program;
- Title V provided grants to the states for aid to the blind and disabled.

The Social Security Act created a radically new role for the federal government. Congress previously had provided subsidies for state and local assistance programs, but this was the first time programs had been established that would be run by the federal government (Social Security) or in partnership with the states (ADC).

As radical a departure as the Social Security Act was, its benefits were originally quite modest. Benefits under Social Security were extended only to those aged who worked in certain occupations and industries, and payments were delayed until 1942. It was not until 1950 that half the aged received any benefits under the program. Until then only orphans and poor children received assistance from the ADC program, and these benefits were also extended very slowly. In 1950 the program was changed to Aid to Families with Dependent Children (AFDC), allowing benefits to one parent (normally the mother) in a family with eligible children.

With the passage of the Social Security Act of 1935, the United States became the last major industrial nation to develop a national welfare program—one that by European standards was quite modest. Three features of the act had long-term and significant consequences for U.S. social welfare programs. First, benefits under the various social security titles were designed for only a select category of the needy. Even as social welfare programs expanded greatly in the 1960s and early 1970s, they continued to be categorical rather than universal, as they are in many other nations. The implications of this design feature will be examined in more detail in Chapter 5.

Second, some of the social security titles allowed the states to determine who would receive assistance and how much they would receive. As AFDC expanded to become the nation's primary cash assistance program for the needy, this feature remained. As will be detailed below, variations in state payments under AFDC are huge, with some states providing much more generous assistance than others. Titles I and V also allowed a great deal of local autonomy in funding assistance to the aged and blind. Until these titles were superseded by the Supplemental Security Income (SSI) program in 1974, funding variations by state were substantial.

Last, the Social Security Act did not include health insurance. By 1935 most other Western industrial nations already had health insurance programs. Roosevelt considered including health insurance in the Social Security Act but eliminated it because opposition from the American Medical Association and southern congressmen was so intense.

State control over the benefit levels under Titles I, II, IV, and V of the Social Security Act substantially limited growth in these programs through the 1950s. In 1960 only 803,000 families were receiving benefits under AFDC, and only 144,000 blind or disabled citizens were receiving assistance under Title V. Thus, by 1960, twenty-five years after the original act, U.S. welfare programs were still extremely modest, and, as events would prove, poverty was still very severe.

The Civil Rights Movement

Just as the Great Depression had served as the necessary catalyst for the nation's first major social welfare programs, the civil rights movement and the ghetto riots of the 1960s served as the stimulus for the next substantial expansion of the welfare state. The civil rights movement, which matured in the late 1950s and early 1960s, centered attention on the economic conditions of millions of U.S. citizens. Civil rights workers often charged that many U.S. citizens of all races were ill-housed, ill-clothed, medically neglected, malnourished, and even suffering from hunger. Most of the nation's public leaders simply dismissed the latter suggestion, but slowly the evidence of acute poverty, malnutrition, poverty-related disease, and even starvation began to be documented.

In 1967 the Senate Subcommittee on Employment, Manpower, and Poverty held hearings on U.S. poverty. The testimony of many civil rights leaders contained graphic allegations of acute hunger in the South. This testimony stimulated two liberal members of the subcommittee—Robert Kennedy (D., N.Y.) and Joseph Clark (D., Penn.)—personally to tour the Mississippi delta. They returned to Washington to testify to the presence of severe hunger and malnutrition in the areas they visited.

The subcommittee's initial investigation also had encouraged the Field Foundation to send a team of doctors to Mississippi to investigate the health of children in Head Start programs. The team issued a report documenting extensive poverty, poverty-related diseases, and malnutrition among the children and their families (Kotz 1971, 8–9).

The most dramatic documentation of U.S. poverty was yet to come. In the mid-1960s the Field Foundation and the Citizens' Crusade against Poverty formed the Citizens' Board of Inquiry into Hunger and Malnutrition in the United States. After on-site investigations and hearings, the Citizens' Board reported its findings in late 1967 and 1968. The findings confirmed the worst suspicions of welfare reform advocates. Investigators had discovered within the larger population of the United States a population that might best be described as an underdeveloped nation. They reported ''concrete evidence of chronic hunger and malnutrition in every part of the United States where we have held hearings or conducted field trips'' (Citizens' Board of Inquiry 1968, iv).

These findings contributed to pressures on Congress for improvements in and expansion of welfare programs. Leaders of the civil rights movement continued to lobby for new programs for the poor, and their arguments were bolstered by the outbreak of hundreds of riots in U.S. cities between 1965 and 1969 (Downes 1968). Many conservatives saw the riots as evidence of a breakdown of morals in American society and an attack on the nation's institutions (Hahn and Feagin 1970). In the final analysis, however, most conservative members of Congress agreed with liberal members that expanding social programs would lower tensions and help restore order. Thus, with the cities on fire and media attention focused on the struggles of the black population and the poverty of millions of U.S. citizens, Congress passed major civil rights acts in 1964, 1965, and 1968. It also expanded existing welfare programs and created new ones. The changes included:

- A 1961 amendment to the AFDC title allowing states to provide benefits to two-parent families where both parents were unemployed (less than half the states adopted this option).
- Formal establishment of the Food Stamp program in 1964 (initially, only twenty-two states opted to participate).
- Enactment of the Medicare and Medicaid programs in 1965.
- Adoption by Congress in 1971 of national standards for the Food Stamp program (the program was not extended to all states until 1974).
- Passage of the Supplemental Security Income (SSI) program in 1972, effective in 1974.

By 1975 five new titles had been added to the original Social

Security Act, and the original titles had been expanded through amendments.

The 1960s and early 1970s, then, saw the second significant installment in the development of American social welfare programs. It is doubtful that anything short of serious civil strife could have produced such drastic changes.

Systemic and Philosophical Limitations on the Welfare State

Why has the United States lagged behind other major Western industrial nations in the creation of social welfare programs? It is certainly not that the country lacks adequate financial resources, or that its tax burden is too high, or that public needs are less. America is rich, its tax rate is low compared to those in other Western nations, and its rate of poverty is high, both absolutely and comparatively (Rodgers 1982, 1–13). There are, however, at least three major differences between the United States and the other leading Western industrial nations that yield some insights.

The first is philosophical. America has a stronger commitment to individualism and free enterprise than is typical of other Western industrialized nations. The country's two major political parties basically support these principles, and there are no significant third parties that promote other principles. Single-member congressional districts and the electoral college system have the effect of limiting the growth of third parties that might challenge the established public philosophy.

Second, America's fragmented power structure makes the passage of nontraditional and nonincremental public policies very difficult. In the parliamentary systems of Europe the executive's party or coalition is in control of both the executive branch and the legislative branch, and disciplined parties generally ensure support for the executive's policies. In the United States, by contrast, power is split between the executive and legislative branches, Congress itself is divided into two competing houses, and party membership need not indicate support for the party platform. The result is that it is very difficult to achieve consensus on major policy objectives. Public policy in the United States is generally a short-term compromise between competing interest groups, designed to meet only limited, sometimes conflicting, and almost always incremental goals. Power is so fragmented that small, entrenched groups from the major parties can often veto even modest, incremental policies. Thus, it has generally been the case that only a crisis, or the perception of one, will precipitate significant change in major public policies—even significant incremental change.

Third, in the United States working-class and low-income citizens have less political clout than their counterparts in Western Europe, in part because the Americans are politically less mobilized. The traditional institutions that play such an important role in educating and mobilizing the working-class electorate in Europe, such as labor unions and political parties, are relatively weak in the United States. The result is what Burnham has called a "hole in the electorate"—the absence of the type of voters who support social welfare programs and left-wing movements in other Western nations (Burnham 1980).

Fragmented political power and a poorly mobilized working class give the economic elite a great deal of power in the American political process (Alford 1975). Political administrations change, but the economic elite is enduring, rich in resources, and politically mobilized. Through its agents in public office and its influence on other public figures, this elite can generally veto public policies that deviate too dramatically from the status quo, conflict too drastically with prevailing capitalist principles, or impose too many costs on business. The business elite particularly objects to welfare programs because they increase the tax burden, reduce the financial incentives or other imperatives to work (especially for low wages), and sometimes mobilize the poor.

Characteristics of the American
Welfare System

These systemic and philosophical factors have obvious impacts on the design of American welfare programs. Basically, welfare programs in the American system are viewed as a necessary evil. They are necessary to control disorder, and as a paean to the fundamental decency of American society and capitalism. Thus, assistance is given grudgingly, in a form that makes clear that it is charity, and only to those among the poor who are considered the legitimate poor—the aged, some unemployed parents and their children (mostly female-headed families), and the handicapped and disabled. Aid to these groups is means-tested, designed to be modest, and, if possible, temporary. Assistance even to mothers and their children is generally designed not to prevent or end their poverty but to serve as temporary, transitory aid to see the family through a rough period. Under existing programs the conditions that make the mother poor—lack of job skills, employment, transportation, or child care—receive scant attention.

Since poverty is generally considered to be the result of personal rather than systemic malfunctions, the state of poverty is considered an illegitimate condition. A poor person is suspected of sloth, moral corruption, or personal shortsightedness; and it is feared that aiding those who become poor only encourages such behavior. The economy is thought to be basically sound and dynamic enough to meet the needs of all but the most disabled citizens, so that furnishing aid to the healthy poor and their offspring only burdens the economy, keeping it from being as profitable and prosperous as it could be. Thus, welfare programs are essentially seen as parasitic on the economy and unaffordable when economic conditions are particularly bad. It is precisely when poverty is highest that more and more public officials demand the reduction or even termination of welfare assistance. As will be detailed below, the Reagan administration has fit this pattern.

The results of the American approach to welfare are obvious. Aid is kept categorical (only specific groups among the poor are given aid), assistance is given as charity (rather than in the universal forms that are common in Europe), and poverty remains high. Even when benefit levels are raised, as they were in the 1960s and early 1970s, poverty can increase. It persists and even increases because (1) the conditions that make some people poor are not effectively addressed. High rates of unemployment and subemployment, for example, may be tolerated or even encouraged in an effort to lower inflation. (2) Those who obtain aid often receive too little to push them over the poverty line (this is particularly true of the nonaged poor). And (3) a large percentage of the poor receive no assistance because they do not fit into one of the categories of the poor who are deemed to be legitimate or the "truly needy" (Bureau of the Census 1981, 20).

With this background, a more in-depth examination of the specific welfare programs available to female heads of households with dependent children may be conducted.

Welfare Programs for Female-Headed Families

In one sense female-headed families with children are fortunate, for they are among the categories of people—along with the aged, disabled, and blind—who are considered the "legitimate" poor. Consequently, if they fall below federal and state income and asset levels, these families can generally qualify for public assistance. Impoverished nonaged single adults (especially males), nonaged couples (especially those without children), and male-headed families generally have great difficulty in qualifying for any type of assistance except food stamps. Female-headed families with dependent children receive the majority of funds expended by the federal government for means-tested programs.

Impoverished female-headed families may qualify for benefits from several types of programs. Table 4.1 provides an overview of the nation's major social welfare programs. This table shows the basis of eligibility for each program, source of funding, form of aid, and actual or projected expenditures for fiscal years 1981 through 1985. The programs can be divided into three types:

1. Social insurance programs such as Social Security, Medicare, and unemployment compensation. Social insurance programs are based on employee and/or employer contributions, and benefits are wage related.

2. Cash-assistance programs such as AFDC and SSI. These programs are means tested, with benefits going only to those who meet income and other qualifications.

3. In-kind programs such as food stamps and other nutrition programs, housing assistance, and Medicaid, which provide a noncash service. These programs are also means tested and often have non-income-related qualifications that must be met by recipients.

As the figures in Table 4.1 make clear, the three social insurance programs are by far the most expensive of all social welfare programs. Strictly speaking, they are not welfare programs because recipients contribute to the programs during their working years and receive benefits related to contributions. Female-headed families may receive benefits from these programs as a result of unemployment, or as spouses and children of deceased or disabled workers who had earned coverage.

The two means-tested cash assistance programs are designed for the poor. AFDC and SSI were projected to cost the federal

Table 4.1

Federal Expenditure for Selected Social Welfare Programs

Program	Basis of eligibility	Source of income	Form of aid	1981	1982	1983	1984	1985
		Social insurance programs						
Social Security	Age, disability, or death of parent or spouse; individual earnings	Federal payroll tax on employers & employees	Cash	145.0	154.1	169.8	179.9	191.4
Unemployment compensation	Unemployment	State & federal payroll tax on employers	Cash	19.6	23.8	36.9	20.7	20.1
Medicare	Age or disability	Federal payroll tax on employers & employees	Subsidized health insurance	39.1	50.4	57.4	66.0	69.7

Cash-assistance programs: Means-tested

Aid to Families with Dependent Children (AFDC)	Certain families with children	Federal, state, local revenues	Cash & service	7.9	8.0	8.2	8.1	7.7
Supplemental Security Income (SSI)	Age or disability	Federal, state revenue	Cash	7.2	7.9	8.7	8.0	9.3

In-kind programs: Means-tested

Medicaid	Persons eligible for AFDC and SSI & medically indigent	Federal, state, local revenues	Subsidized health service	17.1	17.4	19.5	21.3	22.1
Food stamps	Income	Federal revenues	Voucher	11.4	11.0	12.5	12.1	11.6
Housing assistance	Income	Federal, state, local	Subsidized housing		7.9	9.4	10.1	10.9
Child nutrition	Income	Federal	Free or reduced-price meals		3.0	3.2	3.4	3.6
Women, Infants Children (WIC)	Mothers with low incomes	Federal	Vouchers		0.9	1.2	1.2	1.2

government \$7.7 billion and \$9.3 billion, respectively, in fiscal 1985. The in-kind programs are also designed for the poor. They had a combined total cost of \$49.4 billion in 1985. The total projected cost of all three types of programs in fiscal 1985 was \$347.6 billion, about 37 percent of the total projected budget of \$925 billion. Social insurance programs account for 82 percent of the total cost of these major social welfare programs, with cash assistance programs accounting for 5 percent and in-kind programs accounting for the other 13 percent. The means-tested cash and in-kind programs combined account for only about 5 percent of the total federal budget.

A recent study by the Bureau of the Census (1985c, 5) found that of the 6.1 million female-headed families with children and no husband present in 1984, 70 percent received benefits from one or more means-tested or non-means-tested program. Sixty-two percent received benefits from a means-tested program, and 22 percent participated in a non-means-tested program.

Table 4.2 breaks the figures down by program. About a third of all the female-headed families received benefits from the AFDC program. Roughly 38 percent of the families had Medicaid coverage, and about 40 percent had children receiving free or reduced-price school meals. More than 39 percent received food stamps, and 17.5 percent lived in public or subsidized housing.

Many of the qualifying families receive benefits from more than one program. Ninety percent of the 3.9 million households receiving AFDC or other cash assistance received benefits from two or more means-tested noncash programs, and one-third received benefits from four or more programs. All AFDC families qualify for Medicaid, and many also qualify for food stamps. These families may also be eligible for subsidized housing and reduced-price school meals for their children.

Funding for means-tested programs has been reduced

Table 4.2

Participation in Means-tested and Non-means-tested Programs

	Female households, no husband present, own children under 18 years	
	Number	Percent distribution
Total	6,063	100%
Received benefits from:		
One or more government programs	4,232	69.8
One or more non-means-tested programs	1,307	21.6
Soc. Sec. or Railroad Retirement	752	12.4
Unemployment compensation	189	3.1
One or more means-tested programs	3,740	61.7
AFDC or other cash assistance	2,017	33.3
SSI	226	3.7
Food stamps	2,397	39.5
Free or reduced-price school meals	2,400	39.6
Medicaid	2,285	37.7
Public or subsidized rental housing	1,058	17.5
Did not receive benefits	1,832	30.2

Non-means-tested programs include Social Security, railroad retirement, medicare, unemployment compensation, workers' compensation, VA compensation, Black Lung benefits, state temporary sickness or disability benefits, foster child care, and educational assistance.

Source: Bureau of the Census (1985) "Economic Characteristic of Households in the United States: First Quarter, 1984," *Current Population Reports*, series P-70, no. 3, p. 4.

substantially under the Reagan administration (CBO 1983; Danziger 1982; Danziger and Haveman 1981; Gottschalk 1981; SCCYF 1984, 80). When Reagan's massive tax cuts and huge defense expenditures created a serious revenue shortfall and thus huge deficits, the president convinced Congress that welfare programs had to be cut. Eligibility standards were tightened, and funding for many programs was reduced. The result was that between 1980 and 1985 some 4 million people were dropped from means-tested programs. Three million people were dropped from the Food Stamp rolls, and 95 percent of those remaining eligible had their benefits reduced. Some 350,000 families, including 1.5 million children, lost AFDC benefits. Thirty-six states dropped mothers of three with earnings of $5,000 a year or more. Thirteen states set the cutoff level for families of four at $3,000. Three million children lost their eligibility for the school lunch program; almost one million women and children lost their Medicaid coverage.

A recent congressional study found that real expenditures for poor children and their guardians dropped substantially between 1973 and 1983 (Ways and Means 1985, 177). Despite the fact that the number of poor children increased by over 30 percent during this period, expenditures, adjusted for inflation, dropped about 6 percent.

There is evidence that this trend will continue. A resident scholar at the American Enterprise Institute has calculated that in 1988 the share of all federal funding going to non-means-tested programs will be about 40 percent, the same as in 1980. However, funding for means-tested programs will drop from 13.3 percent in 1980 to about 9 percent in 1988 (SCCYF 1984b, 80–83). He concluded that "You can look at that fall as 4.5 percentage points or as a decline of about a third in the share of our federal budget going to low-income programs. . . . I think it will be particularly harsh on near-poor and working poor families."

Aid to Families with Dependent Children

The core cash-welfare program for the poor is AFDC. All states plus the District of Columbia, Puerto Rico, Guam, and the Virgin Islands offer AFDC to one-parent families, with twenty-three jurisdictions also offering assistance to some two-parent families under the optional AFDC-UF (Unemployed Father) program. Primarily, AFDC provides benefits to female-headed households with no husband present. About 80 percent of all AFDC families are headed by the mother, with other relatives of children—grandparents, aunts, uncles—heading another 10–13 percent. Eligibility for AFDC-UF is very restrictive, the result being that only about 7 percent of all AFDC families are headed by an unemployed male.

Table 4.3 provides an overview of the AFDC program, showing the increases in recipients and costs (both state and federal) between 1936 and 1984. The number of recipients grew very slowly until the mid-1960s, then doubled in just five years, and almost doubled again by 1975. Between 1975 and 1983 the number of recipients increased only modestly despite significant increases in poverty and the number of female-headed families.

Table 4.3 also shows the costs of the AFDC program in real (inflation-adjusted) dollars since 1936. The data show that funding for the program has not kept up with inflation. In 1983 the average monthly payment to each AFDC recipient ($107.20) was less than it had been in 1967 ($112.41). The data, in fact, show declining family and recipient benefits of significant proportions over the years. In a recent book Charles Murray (1984) argued that since 1970 poverty has increased, despite increases in welfare benefits and costs. Murray's analysis is flawed, however, by the use of current rather than constant dollars. The constant dollar figures in Table 4.3 show that one reason for the increases in poverty during the late 1970s and early 1980s was reduced funding for the nation's major cash-welfare program. These reductions meant that millions of newly impoverished families who needed assistance were denied it, while families and individuals receiving aid had their benefits reduced.

In 1983 about 3.6 million families participated in the AFDC program each month. On average in the 1970s and early 1980s about 70 percent of the recipients were children. The primary reason children become eligible for AFDC is that their fathers

Table 4.3

Aid to Families with Dependent Children (AFDC)

Cal. year	Avg. monthly number of recipients (in 1,000s)			Amt. of payments			Constant 1983 dollars		
	Families	Total	Children	Total (in 1,000s)	Mo. avg. per Family	Mo. avg. per Recip.	Total (in 1,000s)	Mo. avg. per Family	Mo. avg. per Recip.
1936	147	534	361	$49,678	$28.15	$7.75	$357,203	$202.41	$55.73
1940	349	1182	840	133,770	31.98	9.43	950,404	227.21	67.00
1945	259	907	656	149,667	48.18	13.75	828,583	266.73	76.12
1950	644	2205	1637	551,653	71.33	17.64	2,283,124	295.21	73.01
1955	612	2214	1673	617,841	84.17	23.26	2,298,800	313.17	86.54
1960	787	3005	2314	1,000,784	105.75	27.75	3,366,786	355.76	93.36
1961	869	3354	2587	1,156,769	110.97	28.74	3,852,454	369.57	95.71
1962	931	3676	2818	1,298,774	116.30	29.44	4,277,640	383.05	96.96
1963	947	3876	2909	1,365,851	120.19	29.36	4,444,601	391.11	95.54
1964	992	4118	3091	1,510,352	126.88	30.57	4,851,335	407.55	98.19
1965	1039	4329	3256	1,660,186	133.20	31.96	5,242,323	420.60	100.92
1966	1088	4513	3411	1,863,925	142.83	34.42	5,772,173	438.48	105.67
1967	1217	5014	3771	2,266,400	155.19	37.67	6,762,938	463.09	112.41
1968	1410	5705	4275	2,849,298	168.41	41.62	8,159,602	482.28	119.19
1969	1698	6706	4985	3,563,427	174.89	44.28	9,684,213	475.29	120.34

1970	2208	8466	6214	4,852,964	183.13	47.77	12,451,629	469.87	122.57
1971	2762	10241	7434	6,203,528	187.16	50.48	15,260,781	460.42	124.18
1972	3049	10947	7905	6,909,260	188.87	52.60	16,454,295	499.79	125.27
1973	3148	10949	7902	7,212,035	190.91	54.89	16,168,830	428.01	123.06
1974	3230	10864	7822	7,916,563	204.27	60.72	15,993,923	412.69	122.67
1975	3498	11346	8095	9,210,995	219.44	67.65	17,050,626	406.21	125.23
1976	3579	11304	8001	10,140,543	236.10	74.75	17,747,437	413.21	130.82
1977	3588	11050	7773	10,603,820	246.27	79.97	17,433,498	404.89	131.48
1978	3522	10570	7402	10,730,415	253.89	84.60	16,386,673	387.72	129.19
1979	3509	10312	7179	11,068,864	262.86	89.45	15,192,958	360.80	122.78
1980	3712	10774	7419	12,475,245	280.03	96.49	15,083,522	338.58	116.66
1981	3835	11079	7527	12,981,115	282.04	97.64	14,220,135	308.96	106.96
1982	3542	10358	6903	12,877,905	303.02	103.60	13,292,172	312.77	106.93
1983	3671	10737	7106*	13,812,699	312.88	107.20	13,812,699	312.88	107.20

*Based on January-June 1983 average.

Note: During the period 1935–1938, a child had to be under age 16 to qualify for AFDC benefits. From 1939 to 1963, a child had to be under age 18 to qualify for AFDC. But for the 16-year period 1964–1980, a child under age 21 meeting the program requirements could qualify for AFDC. Since 1981, a child must be under 18, or 19 at state option, to qualify for AFDC.

Source: Social Security Bulletin, Statistical Supplement, 1983.

are absent from home (84.8 percent) and their mothers cannot support them. Some 21.4 percent of fathers are divorced, 25.5 percent are separated, 33.8 percent were never married to the mother, and 4.1 percent are gone for other reasons. In other cases, children are eligible for AFDC because their father is deceased (2.6 percent), incapacitated (5.9 percent), or unemployed (5.9 percent), or their mother is absent (1.6 percent).

AFDC Benefits

There are no standard cash benefits under the AFDC program. Each state determines the financial needs of its poor families and decides how much assistance families will receive (only Alaska pays 100 percent of determined need). The federal government reimburses 50 to 78 percent of a state's AFDC costs (depending on the per capita income of the state). On average the federal government pays about 54 percent of states' AFDC costs. It sets maximum asset limits for recipients ($1,000), which states may lower. Homes, the equity value of a car up to $1,500 (or a lower state limit), and some items of personal property are generally not counted.

Table 4.4 shows the variations by state in number of AFDC recipients, costs, and average family benefits in August 1984. The average monthly benefit to a family was $332.02, or $114.04 per recipient. Notice, however, how much variation there is by state. Three states—Alaska, California, and Massachusetts—provided average benefits of more than $500 per month. Nine states, all but one of which are southern, provide less than $200 per month. Mississippi provides an average monthly grant of less than $100. Even in the most generous states benefits are rather modest, and some states seem to make no serious attempt really to aid their poor. In thirty states benefits are less than 50 percent of the poverty level. Only in Alaska and Hawaii does the combined value of AFDC and food stamps boost the average family of four over the federal poverty level. In most of the other states the combined value of AFDC and food stamps leaves recipient families far below the poverty level (Ways and Means 1985, 197).

States vary not only in cash benefits to recipients but in the proportion of the poor who are covered. Low-paying states cover a smaller proportion. For example, in a recent year Texas provided AFDC assistance to only 22 percent of its poor children, Georgia covered 39.4 percent, Florida 29.6 percent, Alaska 79.7 percent, and New York 103.8 percent (Subcommittee on Public Assistance 1980, 30–31).

Because of cutbacks an even smaller proportion of all poor families with children are covered by the AFDC program. During the 1970s an average of 83 percent of all poor families with children under age 18 received AFDC benefits; by 1983, only 62.9 percent received such assistance (Ways and Means 1985, 192). Similarly, during the 1970s an average of over 75 percent of all poor children received AFDC benefits. By 1983 only 53.3 percent were covered by the program (Ways and Means 1985, 212).

The states have always varied in support services for AFDC families. Under federal law the states can provide such services as job training, basic adult education, vocational rehabilitation, family planning, child care, and legal aid. In fact, only a very small percentage of families receive any of these services. Even job training and placement is not stressed. Since July 1972, AFDC recipients are required to register for the Work Incentive Program (WIN). This program was designed to help AFDC family heads obtain job training and viable employment so that they will no longer need welfare. As is detailed below, most states have put little effort into job training or placement programs for AFDC mothers (Ways and Means 1985, 361–67).

Legal assistance to AFDC families has always been oriented toward collecting child support from the absent father. This policy has been emphasized since 1975. As a condition of

Table 4.4

AFDC: Families, Recipients, and Payments, by State, August 1984

State	Families (in 1000s)	Recipients (in 1000s)	Payments (in 1000s)	Average payment per Family	Recipient
Total	3,681.8	10,719.4	$1,222,453.0	$332.02	$114.04
Alabama	54.4	152.1	6,014.5	110.64	39.55
Alaska	6.0	15.1	3,415.4	566.21	226.87
Arizona	26.1	71.9	3,411.0	211.21	76.63
Arkansas	22.1	62.6	3,332.1	350.49	53.26
California	542.4	1,588.7	281,266.4	518.55	177.04
Colorado	28.9	84.4	8,935.4	309.15	105.91
Connecticut	43.3	125.1	19,496.5	450.56	155.90
Delaware	9.5	24.8	2,294.7	241.50	92.50
District of Columbia	23.2	60.2	6,220.2	268.28	103.34
Florida	99.8	272.2	21,147.7	211.89	77.70
Georgia	87.5	237.4	16,482.8	188.43	69.42
Hawaii	16.8	52.1	6,756.6	402.75	129.66
Idaho	6.3	17.4	1,640.0	258.80	94.11
Illinois	242.1	735.3	69,313.9	286.27	94.26
Indiana	57.3	163.7	12,855.9	224.30	78.53
Iowa	39.2	122.2	13,291.6	339.11	108.74
Kansas	23.0	67.3	7,144.4	310.44	106.20
Kentucky	60.6	159.3	11,542.1	190.48	72.47
Louisiana	73.4	221.0	12,383.0	168.80	56.04
Maine	17.6	49.7	6,049.4	344.03	121.67
Maryland	70.5	190.7	19,944.4	283.08	104.59
Massachusetts	85.5	235.8	50,626.6	592.08	214.72
Michigan	231.8	711.0	85,203.7	367.56	119.84
Minnesota	49.5	143.5	23,391.4	472.52	163.05
Mississippi	52.3	152.8	4,776.3	91.35	31.26
Missouri	67.2	195.1	16,594.5	246.82	85.06
Montana	7.3	20.3	2,242.8	308.84	110.73
Nebraska	14.7	41.8	4,648.6	316.62	111.15
Nevada	4.5	13.0	841.2	185.49	64.82
New Hampshire	5.7	15.1	1,762.6	308.26	116.51

Table 4.4 (cont.)

State	Families (in 1000s)	Recipients (in 1000s)	Payments (in 1000s)	Average payment per Family	Recipient
New Jersey	126.6	373.0	43,993.2	347.49	117.95
New Mexico	17.8	51.2	5,012.5	280.99	97.97
New York*	369.9	1,109.3	157,132.9	424.79	141.65
North Carolina	65.0	159.9	11,463.0	176.36	71.67
North Dakota	4.2	11.5	1,743.8	417.27	151.16
Ohio	224.8	673.1	61,566.2	273.82	91.47
Oklahoma	27.0	78.4	7,002.2	259.77	89.28
Oregon	26.8	70.5	8,076.5	301.06	114.56
Pennsylvania	189.2	564.9	59,053.6	312.16	104.53
Rhode Island	15.4	43.1	5,293.7	342.77	122.83
South Carolina	44.2	119.0	6,816.8	154.16	57.29
South Dakota	5.8	16.2	1,458.9	253.46	89.89
Tennessee	57.9	151.3	7,245.0	125.04	47.88
Texas	115.6	343.4	15,890.7	137.42	46.27
Utah	12.9	37.6	4,145.6	322.37	110.29
Vermont	8.1	23.2	3,171.1	393.54	136.72
Virginia	58.2	153.4	13,787.3	236.89	89.91
Washington	59.6	163.4	24,754.7	415.28	151.50
West Virginia	32.6	101.1	8,225.8	252.32	81.39
Wisconsin	92.7	279.8	44,715.8	482.38	159.79
Wyoming	3.3	8.7	1,040.9	315.32	119.66
Other areas:					
Guam	1.6	5.9	383.5	237.92	64.53
Puerto Rico	52.7	176.1	5,131.1	97.37	29.14
Virgin Islands	1.4	4.0	222.8	160.25	55.86

*Preliminary estimate.

Note: See the *Social Security Bulletin*, tables M-27 and M-28, and *Quarterly Public Assistance Statistics*, table 10, for public assistance data by program for selected years and months. Caseload data by state may be found for individual public assistance programs as follows: *Social Security Bulletin*, tables M-29 through M-32 (AFDC, including unemployed parent segment, foster care, and emergency assistance) and M-33 (general assistance); and *Quarterly Public Assistance Statistics*, tables 1 through 7 (AFDC, as above except foster care) and tables 8 and 9 (general assistance). In addition, tables 12 and 13 of the latter give payment data by state for emergency assistance and AFDC.

Source: Data are reported to the Social Security Administration by individual states and are subject to revision. These include AFDC-Unemployed Parent and AFDC-Basic segments. Payment data are reported before deducting for child support collections.

eligibility, AFDC mothers must assign their child-support rights to the states and cooperate with welfare officials in establishing paternity of a child born outside of marriage. If payments are collected from an absent father, the first $50 a month goes to the mother, with no reduction in AFDC benefits. All additional funds are shared by the federal government and the states to reduce the costs of the program. Most of the states do a very poor job of collecting child support from absent fathers. Nationally, child support is collected for only about one out of five mothers on AFDC. Many states fall considerably below this average (National Forum Foundation 1985).

Problems with AFDC

As the major cash-assistance program for the poor in the United States, AFDC is fundamentally flawed. The program plays no meaningful role in preventing poverty, nor does it solve the problems of the overwhelming majority of families that come under its jurisdiction. Most families who qualify for the program receive benefits for about twenty-five months. Almost all remain far below the poverty level during their period of eligibility. In 1983 only 4 percent of all poor families and 3.5 percent of all poor children receiving AFDC and/or other cash grants were lifted over the poverty line by these benefits (Ways and Means 1985, 214). About 40 percent of those who leave the program remain below the poverty level, and about a third of all families return to the program one or more times (Bane and Ellwood 1983; Levitan, Rein, and Marwick 1972, 50). When AFDC recipients do escape poverty it is usually through a job independently obtained, by marriage, or by increased support from another family member. A variety of significant deficiencies of the program can be examined in two major groupings—disincentives to work and lack of a family policy.

Employment and Work Disincentives

A major deficiency of AFDC is that it generally does nothing more for recipient families than allow them to subsist below the poverty level. While the majority of mothers are now in the job market, AFDC mothers overwhelmingly remain at home—unemployed and underskilled. In a highly superficial and ineffective way, AFDC and a number of other social welfare programs emphasize employment. AFDC, food stamp, and unemployment insurance recipients, for example, must register for job-training programs and accept available employment or forfeit benefits. About 60 percent of all AFDC mothers are exempt from this requirement because they have children under age 6 or because there is no WIN project in their community. Another 7 to 10 percent of all AFDC mothers are exempt because of ill health or advanced age. Thus only about 30 percent of all AFDC mothers are under any requirement to work, unless some of those with children under 6 voluntarily seek employment (which some do).

But even for those AFDC mothers attempting to participate in WIN, the program has been a modest success at best. The program has been stymied by a minuscule number of job-training slots and very limited funds to provide mothers seeking jobs or training with child care. In the late 1970s and early 1980s less than 200,000 children a year were provided with temporary care while their mothers received job training or entered employment. The states have been discouraged from emphasizing job placement and training because unemployment rates are high and because the programs are expensive to establish, run, and support. If the programs are to be effective, the participants must be trained for jobs that are in demand, and mothers must be given child support during training and for some period after they obtain employment. The states find it cheaper in the short run just to dole out modest monthly stipends.

There is considerable evidence that AFDC mothers do want to work and, if given a choice, will choose work over welfare. Some Reagan-initiated changes in AFDC produced one type of evidence to support this conclusion. Until 1969, an AFDC mother lost one dollar in benefits for each dollar earned by employment. This was a 100 percent tax and an obvious disincentive to employment. In 1969 Congress amended AFDC to give mothers an incentive to work. The 1969 rule change allowed an AFDC recipient to exempt the first $30 of earnings, one-third of all additional earnings, and all job-related costs. These provisions lowered the effective tax rate to 67 percent. In 1981 the president convinced Congress to revise the law. AFDC mothers were given a standard deduction of $75 for work-related expenses, and the $30 and one-third of earnings exemption could be used only during the first four months of employment.

President Reagan wanted these changes made because he does not believe that welfare programs should be used to subsidize low-income employment. In his view, anyone who can be employed is not "truly needy." The changes affected a very small percentage of all AFDC families. In 1981 only 11.5 percent of all AFDC families had earnings. By May 1982 only 5.6 percent of all AFDC families had earnings (Institute for Research on Poverty 1985, 2).

The immediate expectation was that, since the changes would leave working mothers with the same disposable income as nonworking mothers and cause them to forfeit their Medicaid benefits, many AFDC mothers would quit the job market. A considerable number of studies on the impact of the amendments have been conducted (Center for the Study of Social Policy 1984; Cole, Danziger, Danziger, and Piliavin 1983; Danziger 1984; Fester, Gottschalk, and Jakubson 1984; GAO 1984; Human Resources Administration 1983; Hutchens 1984; Moscovice and Craig 1983), and none found any evidence of job dropout. The studies found that the amendments clearly reduced the AFDC rolls (this, of course, was one of

Reagan's intentions), and that the income of those recipients who managed to stay on the rolls was substantially reduced. But women dropped from the AFDC program because of their earnings showed no inclination to quit their jobs, despite the fact that their income declined and they generally lost their coverage under Medicaid.

In the Deficit Reduction Act of 1984 Congress took steps to ameliorate some of the negative consequences of the 1981 amendments. One provision of the act allows the $30 disregard to continue during the first twelve months of employment. Those who lose AFDC benefits because of employment continue to receive Medicaid coverage for nine months, and states may at their discretion extend coverage for another six months (Children's Defense Fund 1984, 1–3).

A second type of evidence showing that women prefer work to welfare has been produced by studies of job programs. A number of studies (for a review see Evanson 1984) have found that women who were single parents were the most successful clients of the Comprehensive Employment and Training Act (CETA) and the Employment Opportunity Pilot Project (EOPP). The Supported Work Demonstration (described in more detail in Chapter 6), which provided AFDC mothers with above minimum-wage jobs and supportive services (child care), also showed real gains for the recipients. Two years after the program the recipients were more inclined than their peers to be in the job market, worked longer hours, and had considerably higher earnings. As Smolensky (1984, 10) points out:

> The gains were particularly large for middle-aged women (aged 36 to 44 at the outset of the demonstration). Only one-third of the women were high school graduates. Fourteen percent had never worked, and 61 percent had not held a full-time job during the preceding two years. Many of these women lost their food stamp and Medicaid benefits along with AFDC, so that only 50 percent of their earnings represented an increase in real income. Clearly, despite substan-

tial disincentives, female heads of households will work if
given the opportunity.

Despite this evidence, the Reagan administration has limited
interest in job programs for the poor. The president convinced
Congress to make sharp reductions in funding for all job programs (from $13.2 billion in 1979 to $4.0 billion in 1983) and
to end funding for CETA. As a substitute he has promoted the
Community Work Experience Program (CWEP), commonly
known as "workfare," and the Job Training Partnership Act
(JTPA). Under "workfare," states can require able-bodied
heads of AFDC or food-stamp families to perform community
service work or be placed in a private-sector job as reimbursement for their benefits. The recipient does not receive a wage;
instead, each hour of work is credited toward benefits received.

The Job Training Partnership Act replaced CETA. JTPA
abolished public-sector jobs, placing the emphasis on private-
sector training programs for economically disadvantaged
youths and adults. Two popular programs, Job Corps and the
Summer Youth Employment Program, were retained under
this act. The program is so new that few statistics on program
participation are available. The first figures released, however,
show that less than 200,000 AFDC heads were enrolled in the
program in 1983 (Department of Labor 1984). By design, the
act allows very limited financial support or child care for
participants. Given the design and small size of this program,
it is unlikely to have a major impact on the employment of
disadvantaged mothers. Chapter 6 discusses job programs in
more detail.

Lack of a Family Policy

The stop-gap, short-sighted nature of AFDC is no better indicated than by its lack of concern for strengthening the family
unit. There is evidence (although it is elusive and controversial) that AFDC rules induce some families to break up and

may discourage mothers from marrying the father of their children (Bahr 1979; Becker 1981, 252; Ellwood and Bane 1984, 1–3; Fuchs 1981; Hannan, Tuma, and Groeneveld 1977; Moles 1979; Moore and Caldwell 1977, 166–67; Ross and Sawhill 1975, 114–120; Vining 1983, 108;) The antifamily bias of the program is quite apparent. Two-parent families are ineligible for benefits in most states. Even in states with a UF program, only a relatively small number of families ever qualify. Thus, a family desperate for assistance might conclude that it cannot stay together. Similarly, a woman might decide against marrying the father of her child (or children) because it would make the family ineligible for AFDC or Medicaid.

As will be detailed in Chapter 5, in no other Western democracy does the welfare system put families in jeopardy because they are poor. Nor are people required to be poor or, even worse, remain poor in order to obtain or retain most needed assistance (Gilder 1981, 153). In fact, other Western nations have designed policies (often quite elaborate) to strengthen the family unit.

In order to be made profamily, AFDC would have to be available to any two-parent family qualified as poor. Additionally, any qualifying family would have to be given the educational, medical, employment, and housing assistance required to create a positive, supportive environment for the family. AFDC falls short on all counts.

Education. Generally, the only method by which mothers can obtain educational services under the auspices of AFDC is through WIN. But, as noted above, the states have shown little interest in running large WIN programs, so that AFDC mothers' educational needs are rarely addressed. Nor does AFDC specifically provide for the educational needs of children. The children in AFDC families may receive some preschool, primary, or secondary assistance, but the program does not require such assistance or help clients obtain it.

The federal government finances about a dozen programs

designed to provide poor, educationally deprived, or handicapped children with compensatory educational services (SCCYF 1984c, 115–55). Most of the funds subsidize programs run by public schools; there are special programs for American Indians, for migrant children, and for bilingual education. Nationwide, only about a million poor and educationally deprived children receive preschool educational assistance and some 5 million primary and secondary students receive compensatory educational services each year, financed in whole or part by federal revenues. Most of the student recipients are educationally deprived, but they are not necessarily officially poor. The federal government does not collect separate figures on educational assistance for poor children, but given the total number of students served, no more than a third of all poor children could be receiving any special educational attention.

Studies indicate that preschool programs for poor children can enhance their futures. The best known of current preschool programs is Head Start. Established in 1965, Head Start was initially hailed as the most innovative antipoverty strategy on the horizon. It was designed to improve the discipline and educational skills of poor children and to look after their nutritional and health needs. Initially the program was designed to serve 100,000 children during the summer of 1965, but enthusiasm was so high that 561,359 were enrolled, most in hastily assembled programs (Steiner 1976, 30).

Evaluations soon showed that most of the early summer programs were not effective. Certainly the initial expectation that a great deal could be accomplished in only one or two eight-week summer terms was unrealistic. Studies did show that the nutritional and health conditions of Head Start children tended to be considerably better than those of children from similar backgrounds who had not been in the program; but educational gains tended to be small, especially for children who had not participated in year-round programs (Mann

1977). The most critical of the studies, known as the Westing-house Report, showed worthwhile gains for students in full-year programs, but only minor gains from the eight-week pro-grams—gains that tended to fade as the child completed the first two years of public school (Cicirelli et al. 1969).

The negative reports convinced Congress to phase out most of the summer programs, a task largely accomplished by 1974 (Bureau of the Census 1981c, 359). The conversion to full-year programs and experience-related innovations in teaching techniques led to great improvements in Head Start's impact. More recent studies of Head Start show very positive results (Berrueta-Clement et al. 1984; Yavis 1982, 21–34). After re-viewing such studies, Bernard Brown (1977, 9) of the Office of Child Development wrote that the studies provide "compel-ling evidence that early intervention works, that the adverse impact of a poverty environment on children can be overcome by appropriate treatment." The studies demonstrated that Head Start is very successful in cutting down the rate of school failure, in improving IQ scores and reading skills, and in helping children gain self-confidence. They suggested that the educational gains do not fade, and that a "sleeper effect" often showed up several years after program participation, with Head Start recipients proving more academically competent even into the junior high school years. The more exposure children had to Head Start, the more gains they made and maintained.

Despite the solid evidence that compensatory programs such as Head Start can greatly improve the educational skills of disadvantaged youths, participants in these programs tend to continue to perform below the median level for all students. Educators recognize this gap as the next challenge that must be faced, and they point to inadequate funding as one reason the programs do not have an even more positive impact.

Funding for Head Start and other preschool programs has remained modest. Between 1975 and 1984 an average of

376,000 children a year were served by Head Start, at an average cost of $704 million a year. By law 90 percent of the children in Head Start programs must be from poverty families. If the unlikely assumption is made that all students enrolled in Head Start in recent years were from poverty families, only about 15 percent of all those qualified for the program by their family's income have been served.

The increasingly positive evaluations of Head Start's impact have restored the program's credibility, and even transformed it into one of Congress's more favored programs. While other social programs were being scaled back in fiscal 1982 and 1983, Congress allocated $912 million for Head Start, about $100 million more than the 1981 allocation. In 1984 funding was increased to $996 million. Still, in that year the program enrolled only 430,000 students, a small fraction of the children qualified by poverty. And, in constant dollars, the allocation in 1984 was less than the cost of the program in 1978 (Ways and Means 1985, 535).

Health Care. All AFDC recipients are qualified for Medicaid, a program established by Congress in 1965. Medicaid is a state–federal program, with varying benefits available to recipients of AFDC and SSI, and, at state option, other medically needy persons. Under the Medicaid program the federal government has established certain basic medical services for AFDC and SSI recipients. If a state will pay for these services for AFDC and SSI recipients, the federal government will share the costs. As with AFDC, the federal government pays 50 to 78 percent of a state's Medicaid costs, depending on the per capita income of the state. The basic medical services that the states must provide include inpatient hospital services; outpatient services; physican services; laboratory and X-ray services; skilled nursing-facility services for persons over 21; early and periodic screening, diagnosis, and treatment of physical and mental defects in eligible people under 21; family planning services and supplies; and nurse midwife services. If the state wants to expand the list of basic services and include needy persons who do not receive AFDC or SSI, the federal government will also pay a proportion of these costs. The optional services include private-duty nursing services, dental services, and inpatient psychiatric hospital services for individuals under 21. As a matter of practice, all states with Medicaid programs pay for some medical services beyond the basics required by the federal government. A few states provide all the supplementary services, while some provide only a few.

There is no doubt that Medicaid has had a very positive impact on the health of the poor. Studies (Miller 1975; Silver 1978) show that the poor have considerably fewer untreated medical problems now than they did before the program went into effect. They also show that currently the poor see physicians about as often as other people. Thanks largely to Medicaid and various nutritional programs, infant mortality rates have dropped by more than half since the program was established. In 1965 there were 24.7 deaths per 1,000 live births; in 1984 there were 10.6.

The most serious problem with the Medicaid program is that participation is largely dependent upon a person or family being poor and qualified for participation in the AFDC or SSI program. But even among the poor, assistance is often not available. In some states 90 percent or more of all the poor can participate; in others, only a small percentage are covered. In 1980 fourteen states had programs that were so restrictive that less than one-third of their poor were qualified for medical assistance. Nationwide, about one-half of all poor children are covered by Medicaid (Ways and Means 1985, 233).

Housing. America has never emphasized housing assistance for low-income and poor families. Most of the money spent by the federal government on housing (much of which takes the form of tax breaks) is designed to subsidize the private market, and thus benefits mostly middle-income and wealthy families (Leichter and Rodgers 1984, 285). Less than 1 percent of the total federal budget is devoted to housing programs for low-income and poor citizens (Milgram 1984). One housing specialist calculated that

> since the first payment for low-income housing in the 1930s, all federal outlays through Housing and Urban Development and its predecessor agencies has been $26 billion. The cost of housing subsidies, through the tax system in 1980 alone was more than the entire cumulative amount that the federal government has ever spent for providing housing assistance for low-income people. (SCCYF 1984b, 87)

It is not surprising, then, that only a very small percentage of all American households live in public or subsidized rental housing. In 1984 for example, 3.6 million households, or 4.3 percent of the total, lived in free or subsidized housing (Bureau of the Census 1985c, 4).

About 20 percent of all AFDC families receive housing assistance under one of the government's housing programs (Leichter and Rodgers 1984, 265–87). This means that AFDC families are more fortunate than other types of poor families. It has been estimated that only about one out of eight poor families receives housing assistance (Ways and Means 1985, 329). Some of the housing that AFDC families do receive is of very poor quality, and much of it is located in undesirable neighborhoods. These poverty pockets characteristically have high crime rates, poor-quality schools, limited public transportation, and few good jobs.

The income-qualified but unserved poor population is quite large. In recent congressional testimony (SCCYF 1984b, 71) it was observed that the "poorest of the poor in need of housing assistance number 29 million, including more than 11 million children and 4 million elderly." Millions of families who qualify for assistance but receive no aid are on waiting lists.

Most major cities have a waiting period for assistance of several years. In New York City there is a waiting list of eighteen years for public housing (*Congressional Quarterly* 1982, 1471).

Nutrition. Almost all AFDC families receive nutrition assistance. About 82 percent of all AFDC families receive food stamps. The food stamp allocation is based on income and asset limitations. Qualifying families on average received about $43 worth of stamps per month per recipient or $115 per family in 1984. The stamps can be redeemed at retail outlets for food only. Tobacco, alcoholic beverages, wax paper, soap, and other nonfood items cannot be purchased.

Since the food stamp program is national in scope and stamp allocations vary with income, until recently some of the inequities of the AFDC program were overcome. Families living in states that pay low AFDC cash benefits could obtain more stamps than could families living in states that pay higher benefits. However, in 1981 Congress voted to allow states to count food stamp benefits as income and therefore to lower AFDC cash payments, although this may leave families short of the necessary cash to cover housing, transportation, clothing, and other needs.

The food stamp allotment, unlike AFDC payments, increases with the cost of living. It is based on the current market cost of foods that meet the Department of Agriculture's nutritional standards and are included in their thrifty food plan. If increases are warranted by market changes, adjustments are made once a year. However, since overall funding for the program has been declining in real terms, assistance per poor recipient has not increased since 1975 (Ways and Means 1985, 182).

There are two additional nutritional programs for which AFDC families often qualify. In 1984, 49 percent of all AFDC families received free or reduced-price school meals. Under the school meal programs, free meals are provided to children whose family income is less than 130 percent of the poverty level and reduced-priced meals are made available to children in families with incomes in the 130 to 185 percent range. The federal government spent about $3 billion on school meal programs in 1984, serving about 23 million children.

Sixteen percent of all AFDC families also received benefits under the Supplemental Feeding Program for Women, Infants and Children (WIC) which was established in 1972. This program provides supplemental food to low-income postpartum and nursing mothers and children below the age of 6 who are diagnosed as being at nutritional risk. Sometimes the families receive supplemental foods but generally they are given vouchers that can be redeemed at retail outlets for specific food items required to meet their nutritional needs—for example, dairy products, cereals, fruits and vegetables. In the early 1980s the average monthly benefit to a recipient family was about $30.

The WIC program served 3.1 million women, infants, and children in 1984, at a cost of $1.4 billion. It has been estimated that of those qualified by income for the program, only one-third of the women, one-half of the infants, and one-fifth of the children are served (Ways and Means 1985, 260).

There is solid evidence that the various nutrition programs have had a very positive impact on the health of recipients. Evaluations of the WIC program credit it with reducing the number of children born with low birth weight, a condition linked to birth defects and increased probability of infant mortality (Ways and Means 1985, 260). There is also good evidence that the Food Stamp program has had beneficial effects. In 1977 the Field Foundation sent a team of doctors into the nation's poorest counties to determine if the conditions of the poor had improved since the 1960s. The team reported very significant improvements in the nutrition and health of poor Americans. Most of the poor still lived in inadequate housing and still had far too few resources or opportunities for improvements, but unlike in the 1960s, they were much less often hungry and malnourished: "The facts of life for Americans living in poverty remain as dark or darker than they were ten years ago. But in the area of food there is a difference. The Food Stamp program, the nutritional component of Head Start, school lunch and breakfast programs, and to a lesser extent the Women-Infant-Children (WIC) feeding programs have made a difference." Or, as another Field Foundation doctor said, "Poverty is rampant but the Food Stamp program brings food into the most terrible situations" (Kotz 1979, 9).

As positive as the impact of the Food Stamp program has been, some problems still exist. First, some families still do not receive enough vouchers to purchase all the food they need. The modesty of AFDC benefits aggravates this problem. A Congressional Budget Office study (CBO 1977, 51) estimated that about 57 percent of each food stamp dollar is used to purchase additional food, while 43 percent simply frees money for other family needs. The family could devote a larger percentage of its cash income to food expenditures if AFDC benefits were more adequate.

Second, many poor families find it difficult or impossible to obtain food stamps. In rural areas the poor often cannot apply because the food stamp center is too far away. In both rural and urban areas millions of very low-income families cannot qualify because of income and asset limitations. The asset limit is set at $1,500; the income limit is the poverty line for the size and type of family. Unless the family's net income is below this level it cannot obtain food stamps. A family can be in serious financial trouble but still be above the poverty line. Additionally, if its gross income is more than 30 percent above the poverty line, a family is automatically disqualified regardless of any disasters (such as the loss of a job) that may befall it. Finally, food stamp regulations are generally enforced so rigorously as to discourage many poor families who find the endless demands for receipts and documentation to be a form of harassment. The Field Foundation doctors found that an adversary relationship often develops between applicants and case workers who are under pressure to eliminate fraud. Many applicants find the application and certification process so frustrating and humiliating that they simply abandon their efforts to obtain assistance.

During the early 1980s these problems were compounded by high rates of unemployment and the Reagan-inspired cuts in social programs. The result was evidence of increasing hunger and malnutrition, especially among children and the elderly. Studies submitted to the House Select Committee on Hunger (1985, 25) in May 1985 showed that because of cutbacks in AFDC, food stamps, and the school lunch program, one third of the gains made against hunger and malnutrition in the 1960s and 1970s have been wiped out.

Family Planning. Neither AFDC nor Medicaid places any significant emphasis on family planning. Nor do other federal or state programs even modestly fill in this gap. The consequences are obvious. Of all the Western industrial nations, America has the highest rate of adolescent pregnancy and abortion. This is true even though the evidence reveals that American teenagers are no more sexually active than their European peers (Jones et al. 1985, 53, 54).

As noted above, there is a well-documented link between single parenting and poverty (especially for women who become mothers while they are teenagers). One study based on a computer simulation concluded that cutting the rate of teenage pregnancy by half would lead to a 25 percent reduction in the costs of AFDC by 1990 (Wertheimer and Moore 1982, 24). Halving the number of children born to teenagers age 18 and under would produce a savings of 12 percent. Despite the obvious link between teenage pregnancy and poverty, family planning is a very controversial issue in the United States, apparently for two reasons. Some conservatives believe that the more teenagers know about sex, the more sexually active they will be. The empirical evidence shows this to be untrue (SCCYF 1984b, 37). Second, the Right-to-Life movement opposes the use of abortions and, in some cases, contraceptives. Family planning agencies provide information about both; moreover, the evidence indicates that family planning reduces the abortion rate by helping women avoid unwanted pregnancies (Forest, Hermalin, and Henshaw 1981, 109).

The opponents of family planning have managed to keep both the states and the federal government from dealing effectively with the serious problems caused by unwanted and unplanned pregnancies and births. Some modest federal legislation has been passed. Some family planning services are financed by the Social Services Block Grant, the Maternity and Child Health Block Grant, and Medicaid. However, the major source of family planning fundings is Title X of the Public Health Service Act, which provides grants to public or nonprofit agencies that agree to establish and operate family planning clinics. In 1982 and 1983 Congress appropriated only $124 million for such services under Title X. Grants were made to 4,100 clinics nationwide. These clinics tended to be concentrated in about a dozen states. Only seven states have vigorously sought federal funds and have tried to establish at least some fairly comprehensive programs (Weatherley 1985, 18). Weatherley reports only 274 comprehensive programs nationwide. Few of the clinics are located in the South, where teenage pregnancy and childbearing are the most prevalent.

The clinics established under Title X are obligated to provide free services to adolescents and women who are poor. The clinics must offer a broad range of family planning methods and services, including natural family planning methods, infertility services, and services to adolescents. In 1982 the clinics serviced about 3.3 million persons, about 34 percent of whom were adolescents. Under a 1981 amendment, the clinics are prohibited from providing abortion counseling or referral to teenagers, and they must attempt to discourage teenage sexual activity (Perlman 1984).

A recent study by the General Accounting Office (1980) found that over half of all sexually active teens either do not use contraceptives or use them only sporadically. The study also found that most adolescents lacked access to family planning. The primary problems identified were lack of adequate funding for programs, a lack of focus on high-risk groups, and poor coordination between programs. Since this 1980 study, funding for family planning has declined.

Clearly, federal and state family planning efforts are too modest. Research findings suggest that the Western European industrial countries have much lower rates of adolescent pregnancy and abortion because they provide early and universal sex education, easily available and unstigmatized access to contraceptives, and supportive health and income maintenance services (Jones et al. 1985). These services, as part of a coordinated package of social policies, could play a very significant role in reducing poverty in the United States.

Conclusions

The social welfare programs available to impoverished women and their dependents are deeply flawed. The programs, individually and collectively, are not designed to prevent poverty or to resolve the problems of the women and children that come under their jurisdiction. The programs ameliorate some of the most pressing problems of the poor yet leave them in poverty with fundamental needs unmet. They may very well contribute to the breakup of families as well as discourage the formation of families.

Chapter 5

Some Social Welfare Lessons from Europe

The major industrial countries of Western Europe have not eradicated poverty, but their poverty rates tend to be lower than the U.S. rate (Beckerman 1979; Commission of the European Communities 1981; OECD 1976). This is especially true of the Scandinavian countries, West Germany, Switzerland, and the Netherlands. The rate of poverty in France is similar to the U.S. rate, and Great Britain has a higher incidence of poverty (Townsend 1979).

The major Western countries are also experiencing increases in the numbers of female-headed families, which tend to have low incomes (Finer et al. 1974; Commission of the European Communities 1982). But almost all of these countries have comprehensive social welfare programs that provide more assistance and security for low-income, poor, and single-parent families than similar groups receive in the United States. Some of the countries do a much better job than the United States of assisting lone-parent families with children and aiding women, married and unmarried, who combine work with parenting. The programs of these countries are the focus of this chapter.

Some Limits of Comparative Analysis

Comparative analysis can provide interesting and even important insights about both positive and negative approaches to social policy, but conclusions must be tempered by caution. Three points should be kept in mind when comparing the successes of various countries in preventing, alleviating, or eradicating poverty. First, social welfare programs are not the only predictors of rates of national poverty. Countries with very healthy economies (especially very low rates of unemployment) have less need for assistance programs. Countries with more complex economic problems may employ imaginative and costly social welfare programs and economic strategies but still have serious problems with poverty. The smaller industrial countries—Switzerland, Austria, Sweden, and Denmark, for example—have healthier economies and less poverty than those with larger populations. These smaller countries may have more success, in part, because they have less complex problems.

Second, just because a particular program works well in one country does not mean that it could be adopted or would work as well in another. The national health insurance systems in most Western European countries, for example, were adopted before health-care professionals became well organized and politically powerful. Since the end of World War II medical associations in the United States have been well organized and powerful enough to defeat proposals for major reform of the health-care system. Neither the Democratic nor the Republican party would seriously consider proposing the creation of a national health insurance program in the United States today.

Third, there is a critical difference between maintaining families at a low-income level and helping them achieve a normal standard of living. Great Britain is an example of a country that uses social welfare programs to maintain large numbers of families far below median family income levels for long periods of time. This approach keeps the families from suffering absolute deprivation, but it does not solve their problems (such as the need for a decent job). Because the productive value of the recipients is lost, this type of welfare system also creates a serious drag on the economy. Modeling reform on Great Britain's approach would be a serious mistake.

The West European Approach

America's approach to social welfare policy is fundamentally different from that of most other Western industrial countries (Furniss and Mitchell 1985). There are three major differences. First, most of the latter emphasize prevention of social problems, including poverty, by mean of such policies as national health systems, extensive housing programs, and child or family allowances. Second, there is a belief that problems are best prevented if the most important programs are universal. Thus, these countries are much less likely to use means tests for program eligibility. Universal programs are not only more effective in preventing social ills, they generally enjoy broader public support and do not carry the social stigma often associated with means-tested welfare programs. Third, many of the countries try to ameliorate social problems by public intervention to keep the economy healthy. The Scandinavian countries, for example, use public resources to keep the unemployment rate as low as possible. Low rates of unemployment play a significant role in ameliorating poverty.

Comparing U.S. social welfare programs for low-income families with those of Western Europe reveals how significantly these differences manifest themselves in public policy. The United States is the only major Western industrial country that:

- does not have a uniform cash-benefit program for poor families;
- restricts cash-welfare benefits almost exclusively to single-parent families headed by women;
- has designed its main cash-welfare program to discourage mothers from working;
- has no statutory maternity benefits;
- has no universal child-rearing benefits; and
- has no universal health-care benefits (Kamerman 1984).

Some of the implications of these differences are fairly obvious. In the United States:

- The emphasis is on dealing with families or individuals after they become poor or seriously ill.
- Assistance is temporary, varies significantly by state, and is limited mostly to families headed by single women who must remain single to receive help.
- Little or nothing is done to move most welfare mothers into the job market, and in fact most are discouraged from seeking work by loss of benefits and lack of supportive services (e.g., child care).
- Poor families can receive critical assistance (e.g., medical care) only if they stay on welfare.
- Most employed women cannot have a child without suffering serious wage loss, or even their job.

The remainder of this chapter examines some major European programs and discusses the insights that might be applied in reforming American social welfare programs.

Child and Family Allowances

Every Western industrialized country except the United States provides a package of cash and in-kind programs to supplement the income of families with children (Kamerman and Kahn 1981). Many countries call this set of programs a "family benefit" package. A central component is the child or family allowance, which can be found in sixty-seven countries (Kamerman 1984; 263). In most of them, including Canada, Belgium, and the Scandinavian countries, the allowances are universal and tax free to all families, regardless of income or family structure. In some countries (e.g., Great Britain and France) they are limited to families with two or more children, and sometimes they are means-tested (e.g., West Germany). The allowances vary by the number of children in the family, and sometimes by the age of the children. France, for example, provides a larger supplement to families with young children. In all the major Western countries a special supplement is provided to single-parent families. None of the countries excludes families from these benefits because they are intact or because a parent is in the labor force.

The allowances were originally designed to increase the birth rate. Whether the grants ever had a significant impact on childbearing is problematical, but they remain popular because they supplement the cost of raising children. By sharing the cost of childrearing the society helps insure that the basic needs of children are met. The general belief is that children raised in a more financially sound environment will be healthier, better educated, and more productive members of society.

The size of the grants is generally small, but the evidence suggests that they are a significant aid to low-income, especially single-parent, families (Kamerman 1984; 263). This is especially true since the allowance is larger when there is a lone parent.

Housing Assistance and Allowances

Governments in Western Europe use a wide range of policies to subsidize the construction, purchase, and rental of quality housing. Their role in housing tends to be substantially greater than that of the U.S. government (Headey 1978; Leichter and Rodgers 1984; McGuire 1981). Many of the West European governments became involved in housing policy in an effort to overcome the destruction brought about by two world wars. Once involved they tended to stay involved. Both conservative and liberal political parties in Western Europe generally support an extensive role for the government in housing. The conservatives believe that government programs subsidize and stimulate the private housing market and the economy, while liberal parties add that decent housing for all should be a societal goal. Quality housing is a national resource because it is a durable good which also provides a healthier environment for families.

The governments of Western Europe use a wide range of housing policies, including public housing, saving bonuses to help families accumulate the down payment for a home, subsidies to builders or nonprofit housing cooperatives, assistance to home mortgage lenders, and housing allowances. Great Britain, for example, stresses public housing and housing allowances. About 20 percent of all housing in Britain is publicly owned. A wide range of income groups live in this public housing, with rents reflecting the size and income of the family. Housing allowances are also used to assist families living in privately owned housing.

In Sweden some 45 percent of all housing was built with public funds, about 20 percent is owned by consumer cooperatives, and about 35 percent is privately owned. Regardless of sector, about 90 percent of all housing in Sweden is financed by the government. This policy lowers the costs of housing, making it generally more affordable. In addition, Sweden has a very generous housing allowance policy. About 50 percent of all families with children are eligible for a housing allowance.

The governments of France, West Germany, and the Netherlands all play a major role in housing. Like Sweden, these countries stimulate the housing market through quasi-public housing—housing subsidized and financed by the government and run by quasi-public authorities. Public and quasi-public housing is not limited to low-income families in these countries; it is commonly occupied by middle-income families. This takes away any stigma on public housing and promotes a healthier housing environment. These countries also use housing allowances to assist families with limited incomes. West Germany and France provide larger grants to single-parent families; the Netherlands and Britain increase the grants to families whose rent is high in relationship to their income.

Single-parent families benefit greatly from the housing programs in all these countries. They are given preference in public or quasi-public housing and receive housing allowances. In some countries they receive a larger allowance to make up for the loss or lack of a second adult earner. In most of these countries the housing allowance, along with the family or child allowance, constitutes a significant income grant to single-parent families. As Kamerman (1984; 264–65) notes:

> If one adds the value of the housing allowance to the family allowance allotted a non-wage-earning mother, the total accounts for almost half of her income in France, more than a third in Sweden, and more than a quarter in Germany and the United Kingdom; for the working mother, the transfers together constitute almost 40 percent of her income in France, more than 25 percent in Sweden, and close to that in the United Kingdom and Germany.

One obvious result of the use of family and housing allowances is that single-parent and other low-income families are much less dependent upon cash means-tested welfare programs.

Child Support

In recent years some countries have adopted a new approach to child support when one parent is absent. Austria, France, Denmark, and Sweden now use "advance maintenance payments" (Kamerman and Kahn 1983). Under this program, all absent parents are taxed a certain proportion of their income each month. The proceeds are accumulated and used to provide a minimum monthly grant to all children with an absent parent. If the absent parent is unemployed or cannot be found or identified, the child or children still receive the minimum grant. An absent parent may also make additional contributions directly to the children.

The advance maintenance payments program enjoys growing popularity, for it has several advantages. First, the policy greatly increases the chance that an absent parent will make regular payments for child support. The program does so not by penalizing the absent parent, but by assessing the absent parent at a fair and regular rate. The burden on the absent parent is often reduced by the monthly tax which keeps the parent from falling behind and then being obligated to pay a burdensome amount to catch up. Second, children are not penalized if the absent parent cannot pay or cannot be located. Third, requiring absent parents to meet their child-care obligations reduces the likelihood that the custodial parent and children will need public assistance.

The advance maintenance approach may work better in the four West European countries than it would in the United States. The reason, as noted above, is that many of the European social welfare programs that support and assist low-income families are universal, with no means tests. By contrast, a single-parent family in the United States often becomes ineligible for health or nutritional assistance when income from a job or child support increases, even very modestly.

Maternity Benefits

Most of the major West European industrial countries have programs that protect the jobs and incomes of women for a period of time before and after childbirth. Maternity leaves are generally covered by the country's social insurance program. This approach assures that a woman will receive the assistance regardless of the wealth of her employer. There is no means test for the program, benefits are in cash, and they are usually wage-related. In most cases a woman receives at least 90 percent of her normal wage up to some cutoff point. The leave lasts sixteen weeks in France and thirty-six weeks in Sweden, but most countries set the leave at twenty-four to twenty-six weeks, allowing for extensions for specified periods if the mother or child is ill (Kamerman and Kahn 1981, 71–73). Some countries allow a mother to extend the leave for a few weeks at her discretion, but at a reduced benefit level. Sweden allows the parents to decide, after the birth of the child, which of them will take the leave.

The social insurance programs also usually allow a mother to take a paid leave to care at home for a sick child. The mother usually receives 90 percent of her normal pay for a certain number of days. If the child's illness is extended, the mother is sometimes covered at the rate specified for personal illness under the social insurance program. Sweden allows either parent to take this leave.

Child Care

The issue of child care provides interesting insights into social welfare philosophy. In many of the West European countries, as in the United States, there has been intense debate about the role that public authorities should play in child care. The family policies or family benefit packages that exist in Western Europe were built on the assumption that most mothers would remain at home until their children reached school age. As women have become more career oriented and formed a larger percentage of the work force, child-care policy has had to be reexamined. A few countries, especially in Scandinavia, have in recent years concluded that women should be given the support they need to be mothers and career employees at the same time (Kammerman and Kahn 1981; Rosengren 1973; Wagner and Wagner 1976; Young and Nelson 1973). This decision reflects the existence of both a more liberal social philosophy and a labor shortage in these countries.

By contrast, other European countries have traditionally encouraged mothers to stay at home with their children until they are enrolled in preschool (around age three). In recent years some countries have accepted the change in women's roles and have begun to develop policies designed to accommodate mothers who want to return to the job market before their children enter preschool or who need child care during nonschool hours. Some countries have established publicly supported or subsidized child-care centers, with fees scaled to income. Only France has created enough facilities to match demand to any significant degree. In West Germany and Great Britain there are long waiting lists for the facilities that have been established and there is continued reluctance about facilitating the return to the job market of women with small children. In most of the countries the mothers must pay for family or center care.

In Scandinavia the governments tend to play a much larger role in providing child care, but facilities are still inadequate to meet demand. The publicly supported centers in Sweden, for example, have long waiting lists. Still, the obligation of providing child-care assistance has been accepted and the facilities are being expanded. In Sweden the public centers are neighborhood based and run by certified child-care specialists. A board composed of center employees and parents sets broad policy and supervises the operation of the center. Fees reflect the salary of the parent, the number of children in the family, and how long the center cares for the child each day. Fees are kept modest to encourage center use, and they are lower for single-parent families. All of the centers have a developmental, as opposed to custodial, orientation. Each child receives educational, nutritional, and health-care assistance. Some centers are open twenty-four hours a day for parents who work nights. Often the centers share facilities with programs for retired citizens who can, if they wish, help out with the children.

In sum, it is in child-care policy that other Western industrial countries most resemble the United States. Although in France and in Scandinavia there has been acceptance of the need for a larger public role in child care, in none of the countries is the demand for child-care assistance currently being met.

Health Care

Most advanced industrial countries in the West—except the United States—have a universal program of national health insurance or a national health service (Leichter 1979; Roemer 1977; Simanis and Coleman 1980). These programs provide comprehensive health care to all citizens regardless of income, age, family structure, or employment status. While all individuals and families have the same benefits under the programs, low-income citizens and families certainly receive a higher level of health assistance than they would if care were based on ability to pay. Additionally, a family struggling on limited income cannot be made poorer by health-care-costs, nor does the family have to be officially designated as poor—and then stay poor—to receive health-care assistance. Thus, the health-care system is one method by which these countries prevent poverty.

All the countries place emphasis on preventive health care, which is considered less costly than an acute health-care approach where people seek medical care only after they become ill. In a preventive system emphasis is placed on health education and on such services as basic medical screening for early detection of conditions that can cause serious illness, maternity care, and prenatal and postnatal care. Most of the countries have networks of neighborhood centers that specialize in maternity and child health care. In France, mothers cannot receive their child or family allowance unless they schedule regular visits to these clinics for themselves and their children.

With the exception of Great Britain, all the major West European industrial countries have national health insurance systems. Under these systems, most citizens become a member of the national health insurance program through their employment. All employers are obligated to enroll their employees in an approved insurance plan that provides comprehensive health-care coverage to the employee and any dependents. Both the employer and the employee pay a monthly fee, which provides most of the funding for the system. Any citizen who is unemployed or aged is enrolled in a health plan financed by the federal and/or local government.

Under national health insurance, participants select a doctor of their choice, who either treats them or, if necessary, refers them to a specialist. The doctors charge on a fee-for-service basis, but the government establishes the reimbursement rate. The patient may pay a small fee for services, especially if medical appliances or drugs are prescribed.

Germany was the first Western country to adopt a health insurance program, the Sickness Insurance Law of 1883 (Flora and Heidenheimer 1981; Sulzbach 1947). Originally the act covered industrial wage earners but not their families. In 1885 and 1886 the law was amended to bring some workers in commercial enterprises and farm work into the program. The program, financed by a tax on workers and their employers, provided medical care, cash sickness benefits, maternity benefits, and a cash grant for funeral expenses. The program was administered by sickness funds, a type of cooperative organization that had long existed in Germany. In 1885 there were almost 19,000 such funds.

During the first two decades of the twentieth century, the program changed in two major ways. Eligibility was extended to more workers and increasingly to their dependents, and benefits became more comprehensive. National standards for the sickness funds encouraged them to consolidate, greatly reducing their numbers. Hundreds of amendments strengthened and expanded the program over the years. Currently almost all West German citizens are covered by the program. Employees make monthly contributions, which are matched by employers. Some of the costs are financed out of general revenues. All citizens earning less than a regularly adjusted minimum income standard are required to participate in the program, and their dependents are automatically covered. Those earning above the standard may participate on a voluntary basis. Pensioners and citizens receiving unemployment compensation are covered by public programs.

Medical benefits under the German program are comprehensive, with modest cost sharing. In addition to comprehensive health care, the program provides sickness allowances, a household allowance so that families can hire assistance during an illness, a lump-sum maternity payment, and a cash grant to cover funeral expenses. Doctors are paid on a fee-for-service basis, with fee schedules determined by the federal government.

The national health insurance systems in other Western industrial countries work very much like the German system. National health insurance is not inexpensive, but it provides comprehensive coverage for all citizens for about the same per capita cost as the American system (Simanis and Coleman 1980, 5).

Great Britain established a national insurance plan in 1911. The initial plan covered workers, but not their dependents. The 1911 act was designed to supplement and, in part, take the place of worker organizations known as friendly societies, cooperative organizations that pooled fees to provide workers with cash benefits during illness, medical care by a contracted physician, and an allowance to cover funeral expenses.

The 1911 act covered only workers earning less than an established income standard. The program was financed by worker and employer contributions and general tax revenues. Covered workers received physician care (but not hospitalization) and sickness, disability, and maternity benefits. The friendly societies were pacified by being allowed to administer all but the medical benefits. By the 1940s only about 40 percent of the population was covered under the act (Leichter 1979, 167).

To overcome many of the inadequacies of this approach, the National Health Service Act was passed in 1948. Under it the government assumed responsibility for financing hospital and clinic construction and for training and hiring medical personnel. Unlike a national health insurance system, the government became the owner of the country's hospitals and clinics and the employer of most doctors and other medical personnel. Some 85 percent of the cost of the program is financed by the central and local governments. Employers and employees pay modest insurance premiums that finance another 10 percent of costs. Cost-sharing and user fees provide the other 5 percent of financing.

Every British citizen is covered under the act, and the benefits are comprehensive. Citizens receive routine medical care by registering with a physician of their choice. General practitioners receive a fee for each patient registered with them. As a cost-cutting incentive, group practitioners are allowed to have more patients than solo practitioners. Hospital and surgical care is provided by physicians who are salaried employees of publicly owned hospitals. Patients pay a small fee for dental and ophthalmic services and for prescriptions. There are normally no fees associated with routine medical and hospital services.

The British Health Service has been plagued by a very weak national economy, preventing the nation from increasing funding to upgrade medical services. Still, the British National Health Service, like the health-care programs found in the other Western nations, provides comprehensive health care to all citizens, regardless of their income.

Market Strategies

Many Western industrial countries use economic strategies to reduce the need for social welfare assistance. One of the most common strategies is the use of economic policies and public programs to keep unemployment as low as possible. Norway and Sweden, for example, have been successful in keeping unemployment below 3 percent (Office of Economic Research 1981, 10). They do so through the manipulation of interest rates, public investments in the private sector, and government job training, relocation, and employment programs (Furniss and Tilton 1979, 134–38). By contrast, American administrations have used economic policies to increase the unemployment rate, as a method of reducing or controlling the rate of inflation.

Keeping unemployment low is often part of a more complex economic strategy. Sweden, for example, has made economic efficiency a key element in its market approach. The Swedes believe that their industry must be modern and highly productive in order to remain competitive in international markets. This means that industry must constantly innovate to promote productivity, and that weak, inefficient businesses must be weeded out. The maintenance of obsolete or inefficient jobs is not allowed because this would reduce efficiency. Workers and unions do not have to struggle to protect obsolete jobs, for workers whose jobs are abolished are assured of other, equally good positions. If the worker needs retraining or relocation he or she receives this help with pay during the transition period. Thus, full employment is part of a larger economic strategy designed to keep the economy healthy, competitive, and prosperous. Sweden recognizes that only this type of economy can produce the surpluses needed to provide a wide range of supportive human services.

Summary and Conclusions

The social welfare systems of other major Western industrial societies differ from the American system in several important respects. First, most of these countries provide a broader core of universal, non-means-tested assistance programs to all citizens. The most obvious example is the package of programs provided to all citizens through the health-care system. Second, the countries have programs specifically designed to assist families with children. These programs are either universal or provided to almost all middle- and low-income families. All the countries make this package available to lone-parent families, with many giving such families a larger supplement. Third, none of them denies assistance to intact families or requires a lone parent to stay unemployed, single, or poor to qualify for, or remain qualified for, critical assistance such as housing or health care. Fourth, the cash-benefit programs are uniform for all poor families, regardless of family structure.

Because of the benefits that citizens receive from programs such as national health insurance, family allowances, varied housing programs, and maternity leaves, fewer low-income families need income-tested cash-welfare assistance. The universal and other broadly provided assistance programs thus increase the security, independence, and presumably the dignity of low-income families, allowing them more options for work, training, or education. France has specifically altered and expanded its social welfare package in recent years to give greater assistance to lone-parent families and to allow low-income women a choice of staying home with their children or entering the labor force. Sweden has designed its system to facilitate management of simultaneous work and parenting roles by both parents.

This review suggests that for several reasons the social welfare programs of Western Europe are better designed than the U.S. programs. First, they better meet many of the basic, critical needs of citizens. This is especially true of health-care and housing programs. The universal financing of such programs as health care and maternity leaves allows all citizens to enjoy these benefits regardless of the wealth of their employer. Second, they do not require a parent to be single or remain single or unemployed to receive needed assistance. These negative incentives are built into the American system. Third, they provide a uniform level of benefits to all poor families, including intact or single-parent families that fall on hard times. There are lessons here that could inform alterations in the American approach to social welfare.

Some West European programs are particularly imaginative and provide cues about how American programs could be improved. Most obvious is the advance maintenance payments program now in effect in a number of countries. Sweden's universally financed maternity leave, which can be used by either parent, and the broadly available housing allowances found in West Germany, France, and Sweden are other good examples.

Last, the market strategy of some of these countries yields a critical insight. The health of a country's economy is the key predictor of the poverty rate. Public policies designed to keep unemployment low, productivity high, and industries competitive, and to support, retrain, and relocate those out of the job market are critical means by which a nation can limit poverty.

Chapter 6

Reforming the American Welfare System

Establishing, updating, or revising welfare programs has never been easy in the United States. As noted earlier, it took the crisis of the Great Depression and the turmoil of the 1960s to produce the patchwork system of programs that we currently refer to as the American welfare system. Richard Nixon tried diligently to reform the welfare system, hoping to substitute a version of the negative income tax[1] for most of the extant programs. His plan was twice passed by the House, but it died

1. In the simplest terms, under a negative income tax system a family's (or individual's) income is compared to a predetermined poverty threshold. If a family's income is above the threshold, it will pay an income tax; if it is below the threshold, the family has a "negative income" and the government will transfer income to the family to bring it up to the poverty level.

from lack of action by the Senate. Although President Nixon's proposal finally failed, it promoted a consensus about the most plausible approach to welfare reform. Gerald Ford made a modest effort to recoup Nixon's momentum on the issue by offering another reform package based on the negative income tax, but he abandoned the effort when the economy turned increasingly sour. Jimmy Carter hoped that welfare reform would be a major accomplishment of his administration. He proposed a system based on a negative income tax for those able to work, and a guaranteed income for those who were unemployable. President Carter's plan also foundered in Congress.

The defeat of Carter's plan cast a pale over reform for most of a decade. The concepts on which that plan was based had been debated during three administrations, and it seemed clear that Congress was unlikely to accept reform based on substantial use of the negative income tax plan. The consensus around which debate centered during three administrations had clearly dissolved.

President Ronald Reagan's idea of reform consisted primarily of compulsory work programs for the poor and reducing or abolishing as many welfare programs as possible, while trying to convince the states to assume a larger share of the costs and administrative burdens of those programs that survived. Equally important, Reagan's tax reduction plan created huge deficits, making it even less likely that Congress would entertain welfare reforms that would raise federal outlays, even temporarily. Last, in the early and mid-1980s there was no generalized crisis of the magnitude that had spawned programs in the 1930s, 1940s, 1960s, or early 1970s. Poverty was increasing rapidly, but Reagan was successful in dismissing this as a temporary aberration of his economic policies.

It would be easy to use the above facts to argue that in the immediate future reform of the welfare system or passage of new programs to help families is unlikely. There are several reasons why this may not be true. First, there is currently a great deal of interest in a number of nonwelfare[2] policies that have the potential to improve the economic conditions of low-income families. The private sector, especially large corporations, is increasingly sponsoring and financially supporting a range of employee programs with significant implications for families. Second, the budget struggles that have taken place during the Reagan years prove that there is solid support in Congress for antipoverty programs. Congress has persistently refused to cut welfare programs as deeply as the administration has proposed, and it has consistently defended the basic social need for the programs. There is also evidence that Congress is currently more interested in reforming existing programs than in replacing them. These reforms would be much less expensive than the major overhauls of the welfare system debated in most recent administrations, and thus they have more potential for passage.

Some of the most obvious nonwelfare policies currently under debate include an array of child-care options, both publicly and privately supported. There is also increasing emphasis on child support enforcement, maternity leaves, better educational standards for all school children, and tax reforms to benefit all low-income households. A growing number of states and cities have passed comparable-worth statutes, a policy supporting equalization of male and female wage levels that has obvious implications for female-headed families. Sex education is another nonwelfare policy that could have the effect of reducing the size and number of female-headed households, and it is attracting renewed interest. There are also proposals before Congress to improve the retirement benefits of women who move in and out of the job market (primarily because of family responsibilities), and women who choose to maintain a

2. As used here, "nonwelfare" refers to government programs that are not means tested and to programs sponsored and financed by the private sector.

household. These and other nonwelfare options will be discussed in more detail below, along with the possibility of reforming the AFDC program, increasing housing subsidies, and improving nutrition and health-care programs. A combination of nonwelfare and reformed or modestly expanded welfare programs could form the core of an improved, if highly imperfect, antipoverty strategy in the United States.

In analyzing these policy options, the critical question is whether a combination of nonwelfare and welfare reforms can adequately address the causes of poverty among female-headed households. Chapter 3 identified a series of correlates of poverty that can be grouped under three categories: the increasing number of broken families, the income problems of female-headed families, and the high unemployment rate of men, especially black men. Potential reforms are analyzed below, and the extent to which they would address the major causes of poverty among female-headed families is assessed.

Nonwelfare Options

There are many non-means-tested programs that could have a significant impact on the economic conditions of families, including those headed by women. These policies would also promote the family by removing some of the major economic strains that prevent the formation of families or contribute to their breakup. The most promising nonwelfare options may be discussed under four major categories: family policies, educational programs, job programs, and comparable-worth policies.

Family Policies

Child or Family Allowances. Scholars who study social welfare programs often argue that the United States should adopt a universal family or child allowance program fashioned after those found in other Western industrialized nations (Kamerman 1984, 270). Even some conservatives (for example see Gilder 1981, 153) have written in support of such an option. Proponents argue that the empirical evidence shows that the allowances promote family life by giving parents more financial security, which in turn creates a healthier, more stable environment for children. In the long run, proponents argue, improved family life promotes a better, more prosperous society less dependent upon public support.

The evidence presented in Chapter 5 strongly supports this conclusion. Yet Congress has never given serious consideration to a universal child or family allowance. In large part, this lack of serious attention results from the categorical orientation of welfare programs in the United States. American policy makers are disinclined to consider programs that would aid all parents or children without regard to economic need. The kind of means-tested child allowance program found in nations such as West Germany might have more appeal. This type of program, however, could be established most easily through reform of the AFDC program or the Earned Income Tax Credit.

Child Support. As shown in Chapter 3, most mothers are not awarded child support in divorce or separation agreements. Those who are generally receive low awards, and most get only part of the support they have been awarded. Many divorced and separated women and their dependents live in, or close to, poverty because they receive inadequate support from the absent parent or none at all.

Two reforms could improve this situation. First, the states could do a better job of requiring identification of the father, seeing that reasonable support is awarded, and enforcing the requirement that the support be paid. One major reason that absent fathers stop making payments is that, once they fall behind, the sum owed grows and they become discouraged about ever being able to make the debt good. States can deal with this problem in part by carefully monitoring payments and using garnishment of wages to keep payments current and the size of the debt in check.

The second reform is more substantial and would draw upon the Swedish advance maintenance plan discussed in Chapter 5. An American version of the plan has been suggested by Garfinkle (Garfinkle and Uhr 1984). First, all parents living away from their dependent children would be subject to a child support tax. This tax would be withheld from the parent's pay, much like the Social Security contribution. The tax would vary according to the number of children. For example, the tax on the first $60,000 in earnings might be 17 percent for one child, 25 percent for two children, increasing to a maximum of 33 percent for six or more. Second, all children with an absent parent would receive a monthly benefit equal to the tax or a minimum, whichever is higher.

The advantages of this plan are obvious. First, all children with an absent parent would receive support—either from the parent or from federal revenues. Second, all children would receive a minimum benefit. Thus, children of a poor or unemployed parent would still receive assistance. Third, the tax would require all parents to face the fact that they will always have a financial responsibility for their children. Last, the program would probably lower the poverty rate for female household heads and their dependents. A demonstration project is currently being conducted in Wisconsin to determine if the plan would lower the poverty rate and produce a net saving. Early reports from the study (Garfinkle and Uhr 1984, 120) suggest that it will result in a substantial net saving in AFDC expenditures.

Child Care. One of the most critical needs of parents who want or need to be employed or to enter educational or job training programs is adequate, affordable child care. The

demand for child care is currently very high and can be expected to increase in the future. The population of children under 6
is expected to grow from 19.6 million in 1980 to 22.9 million
in 1990. The number of children under 10 in single-parent
households is also expected to increase, from 6 to 9 million,
during this period. And, of course, women both married and
unmarried are increasing their participation in the work force.
Currently over half of all single mothers are employed, and by
the early 1990s over half of all married mothers with young
children are expected to be employed (SCCYF 1984a, iv).

According to a recent study by the Bureau of the Census
(1982, 15–19), many mothers report that they would enter the
job market if child care were available. This includes 26 percent of all mothers not in the job market. The figure increases
to 36 percent of women in a household with an annual income
below $15,000, and 45 percent of single mothers. Additional-
ly, 21 percent of all mothers working part time said that they
would increase their work hours if they could obtain child care.

Any reform effort would have to deal with four separate
child-care problems: inadequate supply, lack of knowledge
about options, quality control, and cost barriers. In some parts
of the country, day-care centers have six- to twelve-month
waiting lists. Also, low-income mothers often are uninformed
about publicly or privately financed child-care options. Cost is
a major problem for many families. Studies indicate that care
for one child ranges from $2,500 to $6,500 a year, with the
average cost being about $3,000. Obviously, these costs would
be prohibitive for most single mothers. Quality control is another very difficult problem because child care is so diversely
provided.

There are many ways to address these four issues. In designing any solution, however, it seems inescapable that the federal
government will have to increase significantly its commitment
to child care. Until 1981, Title XX was the primary source of
federal support for child care. It required states to set aside

$200 million for child care. In fact, the states spent about 18 percent of all Title XX funds on child care, totaling about $720 million in 1980. In 1981 the Omnibus Budget Reconciliation Act consolidated Title XX with a number of other programs into the Social Services Block Grant program. Total funding for the combined programs was reduced by 20 percent, and the states were given the option of deciding how much they wanted to spend on child care.

The evidence indicates that the states are spending less under the new program than they did under Title XX (Kimmich 1984, 35). They are spending less because they are receiving less, and because the set-aside was eliminated. The federal commitment needs to be increased. An obvious option would be to expand funding for the Social Services Block Grant and require the states to use the new funds for child-care services. They could do this in a variety of ways, such as subsidizing providers of child-care services to low-income families or providing more lucrative incentives to public or private agencies offering child-care services to specific low-income parents, such as single parents. To make certain that these services were affordable for low-income parents, day-care providers receiving subsidies could be required to use sliding fee scales. Some of the money might be used to match state expenditures on full-day kindergartens in public schools. States might also qualify for matching funds to improve child-care monitoring systems. The states would also have the option of providing subsidies and technical assistance to partnerships between public and private organizations committed to providing more child care for low-income families.

Another option would be for the states to fund startup costs for umbrella organizations that would provide training and certification to providers of family day-care services. The umbrella organization ideally would also monitor family care, provide financial assistance, and develop methods of sharing resources. The providers of family day-care can be given many incentives to cooperate with the umbrella organization, including certification for participation in the Child Care Food Program. Participation in these programs ensures that the nutritional and health needs of the children receive some attention.

Another method by which the federal government could increase the availability and affordability of child care is by changes in the dependent-care tax credit. As currently written, this program provides little assistance to low-income families. Currently, working parents who pay for child care receive a nonrefundable tax credit for each child. For example, for one child the credit applies to the first $2,400 of costs, and for two children it increases to $4,800. The credit decreases with income, with a minimum of 20 percent of outlays for families with a gross income above $28,000.

Most families using the tax credit have incomes over $25,000; only 6 percent of all families using the credit in 1982 had incomes below $10,000 (Ways and Means 1985, 374). Low-income families receive little benefit from the credit because they generally do not have enough federal tax liability to use this option. This program could be altered to increase child-care options for most families. The credit limits could be raised to reduce child-care expenses for most working families. Second, the program could be altered to give larger credits to low-income parents. Last, the credit could be made refundable so that low-income families would receive the full value of the deduction. This last option would provide more assistance to low-income families than to the really poor because the credit would not be received until the end of the year.

Another issue that has to be faced is the growing problem of latchkey children, who come home from school to an empty house because the parent or parents are at work. Estimates of the number of latchkey children vary greatly, but in 1985 the Bureau of the Census estimated the number at 4 million (*New York Times* 1985a, 1). There is growing concern about this problem, but limited action. Many community groups have tried to convince the public schools to provide extended-day programs for such children. Most school systems have argued that even though the idea has merit, they cannot afford it. In Dade County, Florida, however, the United Way has joined with the school district to set up a program that provides afterschool care for 25,000 students. In Houston, Texas, the public school system runs twenty-five year-round schools and eighty-two extended-day programs. Most school systems will need financial assistance from the state or federal government to follow suit.

A positive trend in child care is the involvement of more corporations. Recent figures indicate that about 2,000 corporations are providing child-care assistance to their employees (*New York Times* 1985b 25). The assistance takes a number of forms, including information and referral services, cash grants, vouchers, and on-site child-care centers financed by the corporations. Some corporations have formed consortiums to share the cost of centers and to hire and train personnel to run them.

Corporate involvement in child care can be expected to continue. Corporations are finding that more and more of their employees have dependent children in need of care, and that workers are more productive when they are not distracted by child-care concerns. Corporations are also showing growing concern about the social impact of the neglect children suffer when their working parent(s) cannot afford decent child care.

San Francisco recently passed a novel ordinance designed to deal with the child care needs of workers. The ordinance requires the builders of downtown skyscrapers either to provide space for child care or to pay a tax of $1 for each square foot of space in the building. The city will use the revenues generated to construct day-care centers.

Maternity Leaves. As noted in Chapter 5, the United States is the only major industrial nation without a national policy covering maternity leaves. In most other Western industrial nations women at childbirth are given an employment leave with assurance of job protection and retention of seniority and pension entitlements. In these nations the social security or social insurance system provides the new mother with a cash grant equal to all or part of the wage that she would have received from employment.

The Pregnancy Discrimination Act of 1978 requires U.S. employers to treat pregnancy like any other disability or illness. In practice this means that company insurance must cover the same share of costs that would normally be paid for any illness, and that the employer must give the mothers a short disability leave. The law does not require the employer to extend the leave beyond the immediate recovery period or to guarantee the job security of the mother if she opts for a longer absence.

Many of the nation's largest corporations now extend a twelve- to sixteen-week leave to new mothers, most guaranteeing job protection. Some of these corporations also allow paternity leaves, although most companies actually frown on men who take this option. Many smaller companies extend leaves, but guarantee the mother her job or a comparable job only if favorable business conditions prevail. Most American companies that extend leaves do not give the mother any cash benefits after the immediate recovery period. Some corporations do allow the mother the option of returning to work on a part-time basis.

It seems unlikely that the maternity issue will be resolved satisfactorily in the United States unless a method is found to spread the cost among employers. Only the larger corporations are likely to accept the costs of paid leaves, and in fact many small employers probably could not afford to give their employees paid maternity leaves. Congresswoman Pat Schroeder of Colorado has introduced a bill into the House that would require all companies to provide unpaid and job-protected leaves for eighteen weeks. This program is modest by Western standards, but even so, prospects for its passage are problematical because it seems unlikely that most medium and small companies could afford this policy.

Schroeder's bill might have better prospects if it required employers to make a modest contribution to an insurance plan that would cover the cost of maternity leaves. There are several insurance options. One option is to use the federally supervised unemployment compensation program to cover maternity leaves. A second option is state-managed insurance funds modeled on plans currently run by New York and New Jersey. A third is to require employers to obtain private insurance. Hawaii is currently the only state with such a law. Unless maternity leaves are financed through some type of insurance program, the protection and benefits that most women receive in the immediate future will most likely depend upon the policies and wealth of their company. It should be clear that the lack of a sound policy here will translate into increased welfare costs.

Family Planning and Sex Education. One of the most obvious ways to reduce poverty among women (especially young women) is to adopt policies that help them avoid unwanted and inopportune pregnancies. The evidence presented in Chapter 4 showed that American teenagers of all races have a much higher rate of abortion and pregnancy than do teenagers in other Western industrial nations. This is true despite the fact that the level of sexual activity of American teenagers is about the same as that of teenagers in other Western countries. The difference is that these societies, with more liberal attitudes toward sex, provide easier access to contraceptives and more comprehensive sex education (the evidence clearly shows that students exposed to sex education do *not* have higher levels of sexual activity; see SCCYF 1984b, 37).

Studies from the United States (SCCYF 1984b, 76) show that family planning education for teenagers is more successful if it is conducted within the school system and begins early in the teen years. A comprehensive approach might be based on in-school clinics that provided health counseling, including birth control information and contraceptives, employment counseling, and education on child care and parenting.

General funding by the federal government for family planning also needs to be increased. When President Reagan convinced Congress to cut funding for Title X (which financially assists health clinics that provide family planning assistance) by 13 percent in 1981, 1,000 of the 4,000 federally assisted clinics providing family planning services closed. The empirical evidence clearly reveals that this type of policy is dysfunctional.

Wisconsin recently decided to try to control teenage pregnancy by a totally new approach. The state passed a law in 1985 holding the parents of a teenager who has a child financially responsible for the cost of raising the child. Under the law, state welfare authorities can take either pair of grandparents to court to make them pay the expenses of raising the child. The law was designed to make parents face the financial responsibilities resulting from the actions of their children and, it is hoped, to encourage dialogue about sexual matters between parents and their children. The law also allocates one million dollars for pregnancy counseling, bars a hospital or clinic from notifying parents of a teenager's plans for an abortion unless she consents, and repeals restrictions on the advertising and sale of contraceptives.

The Earned Income Tax Credit. As noted above, many of the scholars who study social welfare programs have argued that the United States should institute a family or child allowance, but the prospects for such a plan are not encouraging at this time. The United States does, however, have a version of a family allowance, which with some revisions could approximate the programs found in Europe.

The Earned Income Tax Credit (EITC) was added to the Internal Revenue Code in 1975. The EITC provides an earning supplement to parents who maintain a household for a child, provided they have an adjusted gross income below $11,000. The EITC is the only tax credit that is refundable. If the parents do not owe any taxes or have a tax obligation lower than the credit, they receive a direct payment from the Internal Revenue Service. This program was adopted to give low-income parents a "work bonus" or incentive to work, and to compensate for the regressive impact of the Social Security tax.

The value of the EITC does not automatically change with increases in prices or real growth in incomes. Instead, Congress has made adjustments every few years. In 1985 the credit equaled 11 percent of the first $5,000 of earnings, or a maximum of $550. Between $5,000 and $6,500 the EITC remains constant at $550. Between $6,500 and $11,000 the credit phases out, with a reduction of 12.3 cents per dollar above $6,500.

The EITC gives low-income families with dependent children some financial assistance, but it is flawed in major ways. First, the credit is not indexed to inflation. Because the adjustments made by Congress have not kept up with increases in inflation, a much smaller number of families received assistance for 1985 than in earlier years. Second, a low-income parent does not qualify for the credit unless he or she earns enough income to provide at least 50 percent of the support of the children in the family. A single mother receiving 50 percent or more of her income from AFDC would not qualify for the credit. Third, the credit does not vary by number of children in the family. Fourth, even those families that qualify for the credit receive it only at the end of the year in a lump sum.

The EITC could be amended in any number of ways to

create a family or child allowance program that could provide much better assistance to low-income parents. Most obviously, the credit could be indexed to inflation, it could be raised from 11 percent to say 16 percent for incomes up to $5,000, a larger proportion of income from welfare programs could be counted, and the credit could be estimated and paid out monthly to low-income families.

Every year since 1980, Congress has debated many potential reforms of this program. Because it is already on the books, and because there are many options for making it a better program, it provides Congress with a viable method of improving the conditions of low-income parents, including single mothers.

Educational Programs

There is probably no single strategy that could do more to break the cycle of poverty than ensuring quality education for all children. Unfortunately, current studies reveal that the education system fails many children. A recent study by the President's National Commission on Excellence in Education found that nearly 40 percent of all minority students are functional illiterates. The commission also found that nearly 40 percent of all students cannot draw inferences from written material, and one-third cannot solve a mathematical problem requiring more than two or three steps. Additionally, in many urban areas 35 to 50 percent of all minority students drop out before graduation (SCCYF 1984b, 37).

As noted in Chapter 4, the educational programs financed by the federal government make a positive but limited contribution to educational gains. The federal programs do not achieve more because they are badly underfunded. Head Start serves only about 20 percent of the children qualified for admission by family income. Also, because of funding limitations, most of the children in the Head Start program attend school only part of the day. Funding for Head Start needs to be substantially expanded.

The federal assistance program to schools with large numbers of educationally deprived children (Education Consolidation and Improvement Act, Chapter 1) is also far too modest. The act provides about $600 a year per poor child. Most school districts use this money to hire remedial teachers, but the assistance is too low to allow the school systems to deal with the problem adequately.

While federal funding clearly needs to be increased, school districts themselves must also do more. A 1985 study by the Committee for Economic Development, a policy research group financed by private business, recommended increased federal assistance plus a number of improvements by local districts. The study's recommendations included better training for teachers, with increased teacher salaries; more attention to low-income and poor-achieving students throughout their school years, with greatly increased attention to the junior high years; year-round schools to give students more attention, extend child care, and give teachers better pay; and a common curriculum of English, math, science, and literature, monitored by periodic testing (Houston *Chronicle* 1985b, 18).

Some school systems, such as Houston and Buffalo, have implemented many of these reforms. Houston and Buffalo have also established a network of magnet schools to offer students a better education in selected career fields such as health care, the arts, science, and math. The magnet schools have proved to be a good desegregation technique, and they significantly improve educational gains. The two major problems with magnet schools are that they cannot accommodate all the students who want to attend, and their funding can drain money away from other schools in the system. These funding problems could be solved by a partnership between private and public sources.

The Reagan administration has proposed to Congress that

the $3.2 billion allocation that annually goes to schools designated under the Education Consolidation and Improvement Act be given instead to parents of low-income students in the form of $600 vouchers. These vouchers could be used to purchase an education in private or public schools. The argument of the Reagan administration is that the voucher system would generate competition between the public and private sector for these students, resulting in better educational opportunities. Critics argue that the voucher would be too modest to stimulate educational options since no school could operate on $600 a child per year.

Job Programs and Benefits

There is clearly no solution to poverty in the United States without fundamental improvement in the employment status of millions of Americans. In the fall of 1985 the unemployment rate was 7.2 percent, little changed from the 7.5 percent rate when Ronald Reagan became president in 1980. A 7 percent unemployment rate translates into some 9 million unemployed Americans, not including another million or so who are too discouraged to continue to look for work (Ginsburg 1983, 29–30). The unemployment rate for minorities and teenagers is a great deal higher than the national average. In September 1985 black unemployment was 15 percent, 2.3 times the white rate. The Hispanic rate was 11.2 percent, 1.75 times the white rate. For Hispanic teenagers the rate was 21 percent, and for black teenagers it was a staggering 41 percent.

As noted in earlier chapters, the high rate of poverty for minorities is often blamed on the breakdown of the family. But the very high rates of unemployment that prevail among young, minority males suggest that many families may break up or never form because a large percentage of these young men are in no position to support a family.

Unemployment is also a major problem of poor female

household heads. In 1983 over 70 percent of poor female heads were unemployed (Bureau of the Census 1984b, 28). If poverty in the United States is to be reduced, major attention must be focused on the employment problems of young men, especially minorities, and women who are single parents.

Although the employment problems of millions of Americans are severe, there are two facts that are quite positive. The first is that the population is aging, and over the next fifteen years there will be fewer young people entering the job market. Specifically, the ratio of people age 29 and under to those 30–64 is falling and will continue to decline until the mid-1990s (Easterlin 1980). This means that the number of new jobs that have to be created each year to lower unemployment will decline significantly, because young workers are new workers. A tighter labor market should also generate higher wages for young workers.

A second positive fact is that since the 1930s the United States has had a great deal of experience with employment programs. This experience has yielded two types of critical information. Empirical studies of the impact of various problems have identified the types of people who benefit most from programs, and the types of programs that work best. The evidence indicates that youths with serious criminal records, former drug offenders, and adults with criminal records have been the least successful clientele (Hollister, Kemper, and Maynard 1984). Teenagers still in school, teenage dropouts without serious criminal records, and women welfare recipients have often benefited substantially from employment programs. The type of programs that work best are those tailored to a particular group that provide adequate training, support, and followup to allow the trainee to get established in the job market. Success is never easy and never cheap. But well-designed programs clearly produce positive results. A few of the programs that have proved worthwhile are reviewed below.

Programs for Teens and Young Adults. Two programs aimed at the one million unemployed youths age 15–24 who have dropped out of school have produced positive results. The first is Job Corps, which has been in place since the early 1960s. This program uses an institutional approach. Teenagers and young adults live in a center away from their neighborhood where they are provided with remedial education and taught discipline and job skills. Currently there are 107 centers with about 60,000 trainees. Many of the young people have arrest records, and about two-thirds are minorities. About half of the centers are private for-profit and the rest are run by state or local governments. All centers are certified and supervised by the Department of Labor.

By 1985 about 1.1 million young people had graduated from the Job Corps (about one-third drop out before graduation). Of the graduates, 75 percent have obtained a job, returned to school, or joined the military. A nonprofit research institute in Princeton, New Jersey, estimates that the cost per student is about $6,244 and is recovered in taxes paid, reduced welfare costs, and lowered crime in about three years (Mallar et al. 1984).

The second program is Job Start. It is similar to Job Corps, but the participants live at home. They attend a school outside their neighborhood, where they receive educational assistance and job skills. This is a relatively new program, currently being tested in ten urban areas. Because housing is not provided, program costs are lower—about $4,000 per student. Early reports indicate that the program has been quite successful in the cities that have had it in place for several years (Manpower Demonstration Research Corp. 1985).

Another recent program that showed excellent results was the Youth Incentive Entitlements Pilot Projects initiated during the Carter administration. This program was aimed at the two million plus teenagers from low-income families who are still in school. The program was designed to get the students into the job market and teach them how to be successful employees. Participating students were given a minimum-wage job on a full-time basis in the summer and part-time employment during the school year. They could keep the job only if they stayed in school and maintained their grades. Between 1978 and 1981 some 76,000 students were hired by private and public employers at seventeen sites across the nation.

A recent evaluation of the program (Rivlin 1984, 168-70) gave it very high marks, especially where minority youth were concerned. Rivlin reported that when the program was made available, poor students—especially black youths—participated at a very high rate. Seventy-three percent of eligible black youths ages 15 to 16 years old participated, and the job incentive was successful in keeping them in school. Under the program the employment rate of black youths equaled that of white youths, and the black youths tended to stay on the job longer. Young black women had an employment rate one-third higher than that of young white women. The evidence from this study clearly suggests that the high unemployment rate of young blacks is not voluntary. Despite the positive impact of this program, the Reagan administration has not been interested in maintaining and expanding it.

Programs for Welfare Recipients. Three programs have had significant success in assisting women on welfare. The first is Job Search Workshops, operational in twelve major cities. The program is designed to help AFDC mothers learn about employment opportunities and how to interview for a job successfully. Some programs also counsel the mothers on how they can obtain supportive services such as child care to help them get established in the job market.

The most controversial program is "workfare." As noted in Chapter 4, this Reagan-backed plan is designed primarily to make AFDC mothers work off the cost of their benefits at entry-level jobs in the public sector. The AFDC mother is given credit for each hour employed, but she does not receive a salary. Workfare projects are currently operational in twenty-three states. In some states a private employer is given a mother's AFDC check in return for hiring her. At least 518 counties were experimenting with the approach in the fall of 1985 (Houston *Chronicle* 1985a, 24). In some counties the program is voluntary; in others, it is mandatory for certain recipients. Critics of this program have argued that it is punitive in spirit, stigmatizes the mother on the job, and fails to give her job training, supportive services, or job benefits. Some public-sector unions have also expressed fear that the program will displace city and county employees.

Many who agree with these criticisms of workfare have nonetheless supported adoption of some version of the program in their states. During the summer of 1985 the California state legislature, which is dominated by the Democratic party, passed a bill instituting workfare. The California bill required job training and child care for participating mothers (mothers with children under age 7 were exempted). A liberal–conservative coalition was formed in support of the proposal because California Democrats became convinced that workfare could work—and they wanted to counter conservative charges that they supported wasteful welfare expenditures.

Many of the states and counties experimenting with the program claim considerable success in placing welfare mothers in permanent jobs and substantially reducing welfare costs. One of the most widely publicized workfare-type programs has been in operation in Massachusetts since 1979. This program has two distinguishing features. First, welfare recipients are given job training or counseling and then placed in private-sector jobs. The state has contracts with 6,000 private sector employers. State officials felt that the traditional approach of placing the recipient in a public-sector job should be avoided because experience indicated that most never obtained a private-sector job. Second, child care is provided for a very small fee ($5 per week for two children) during the training period and while the mother works off the cost of her public assistance. After the mother leaves the welfare roles and while she is employed, child care is still provided at a subsidized rate.

Massachusetts trains welfare recipients to be welders, construction workers, word processors, operating-room technicians, and high technology assemblers. The average pay for graduates of its programs has been $5 an hour. State records show that 86 percent of the women placed in employment have stayed off welfare. Some 20,000 placements have been made, with a saving, after deducting the cost of the employment program, of $60 million to the state.

By the fall of 1985 there was much debate within the Democratic party over whether to propose national adoption of the California version of workfare. The speculation was that a version of workfare might be written into the party's national platform, to help the party make a comeback in 1988. If this were to happen, workfare would become a major national policy option. The critical issue would be whether the supportive services found in the California and Massachusetts plans would be included in any national plan. Without child care and job training, the major impact of workfare would simply be to drive mothers off the welfare rolls. With such services, the program might play a positive role in helping welfare mothers get out of the welfare system, while dealing constructively with some of the needs of their children.

The best-tested and most successful program for welfare mothers was the Supported Work Demonstration. This program provided women who had been on AFDC for three or more years with job training and then helped them obtain a job. Child care was provided to dependent children. Between 1975 and 1980 some 10,000 welfare mothers participated in the program. Extensive evaluations have found considerable value in the program (Hollister, Kemper, and Maynard 1984). Two years after entering the job market, recipients received an estimated $8,000 in benefits over costs. Compared to controls, the program participants had a 20 percent higher employment rate, worked 25 percent more hours, and earned almost 50 percent more. The best results were for women who were 36-to-44 years of age at the beginning of their training. Many of the women in the program lost AFDC benefits, Medicaid, and Food Stamps. Thus, only about half of their earning gains were real, but they stayed in the program. This program provides additional evidence that female heads of households will work if given the chance.

Other programs, including some tax credit plans, have had some successes, but the major evaluations suggest that the programs reviewed above provide the best guideposts for designing employment programs. A major obstacle to more success is the modesty of the programs currently in operation. Expenditures for employment programs have dropped from $14.7 billion (constant dollars) in 1978 to $4.0 billion dollars in 1983 (Ways and Means 1985, 545). In most cities no more than one in ten of those eligible for participation has received assistance. In many cities no more than one in twenty in need has received help. In the fall of 1985 *Business Week* (September 2, 1985, 51) commissioned Northeastern University's Center for Labor Market Studies and the Manpower Demonstration Research Corporation to estimate the cost of substantially lowering unemployment, especially minority unemployment. The studies found that it would cost about $13 billion a year to train some 3.2 million unemployed people, of whom 2 million were members of minority groups. It seems clear that the Reagan administration will not make this commitment, but another administration might decide that ignoring the unemployment problem is more expensive than solving it.

Comparable Worth

As the empirical analysis in Chapter 3 revealed, a major reason female-headed families suffer such a high rate of poverty is that the earning power of women is considerably below that of men. Since the Equal Pay Act of 1963, employers have been prohibited from paying women who do the same job as men a lower wage. The issue of pay equity or comparable worth, however, is more complex. Pay equity involves the issue of equal pay for work of equal value (Gold 1983; Johansen 1984; Remick 1981).

Women who work full time year-round still earn much less on average than men with similar educations and job skills. A major reason is that women tend to be segregated into traditionally ''women's'' jobs (e.g., secretaries, school teachers), and these positions pay less because, historically, employers were allowed to pay women less than men. The rationale for paying women less was that they worked only to supplement their husband's salaries, or to earn enough for some extra luxuries.

Women's groups and many labor unions have been struggling since the early 1970s to overcome the historic pay discrimination against women by focusing attention on the issue of comparable worth. The proponents of comparable worth argue that each job has a value to employers, that this value can be determined, and that it should be the basis for compensation regardless of the sex, race, or social characteristics of the employee. Despite opposition from the Reagan administration, a growing number of states and local governments have passed comparable worth statutes. By mid-1984 fifteen states and some twenty-two cities and school boards had enacted comparable-worth statutes (National Committee on Pay Equity 1984). States such as Iowa, South Dakota, Minnesota, New Mexico, and New Jersey conducted their own studies and concluded that gender-based pay inequities existed and had to be overcome. A number of cities, including Los Angeles and San Jose, have reached similar conclusions. The pattern has been for these states and cities to give extra raises over a two- to four-year period to employees (mostly women) whose salary was clearly less than that paid for jobs of equal value.

Critics of comparable worth have raised three major objections. The first is that the value of a job is highly subjective, and reasonable comparisons cannot be made. In fact, all states, most local governments, and most private companies of any size currently employ such job-scale and evaluation systems. Jobs are classified on the basis of educational and training qualifications and the complexity and responsibility of the position. Second, critics argue that the market should determine the compensation for a particular type of job. The evidence, however, clearly reveals that market forces have been tainted by sexual discrimination; moreover, there is a built-in incentive to maintain this discrimination. Third, critics have argued that achieving pay equity would wreak havoc on the economy—the same argument that was made about ending slavery and child labor. In fact, the experiences of the states and cities that have allocated funds to overcome sexual disparities in pay prove that the cost is usually quite reasonable. Minnesota, for example, allocated $21.7 million over two years, about 1 percent of the state payroll. Los Angeles set aside an extra $34 million to be paid out over a two-year period. The cost to the city of San Jose was $1.5 million. These are reasonable sums that public and private employers can well afford.

Although the Reagan administration, and probably the courts, cannot be expected to promote, defend, or require comparable worth, the movement has a growing momentum at the state and local levels. It seems likely that more states and local governments will develop plans to correct the problem. As they do so, the momentum should increase, and those jurisdictions unwilling to face the issue will be more isolated and exposed to criticism. As women gain better, more equitable pay for their labor, poverty should decrease. One study concluded that if "working women were paid what similarly qualified men earn, the number of poor families would decrease by half" (Sexton 1977, 9). The cited study did not control for job seniority, but it is true that pay equity would have a considerable impact on the economic health of millions of families.

Some Job Benefit Issues

To keep pace with women's changing roles there are a number of relatively small policies that, if adopted, could combine to help families considerably. In the early and mid-1980s a bipartisan group of lawmakers introduced in each session of Congress a package of bills known as the Economic Equity Act. It included twenty-two measures designed to help women workers and single heads of households. The measures included:

- Allowing nonworking spouses to increase their contributions to individual retirement accounts.
- Allowing workers to qualify for retirement benefits after five years of work. Workers could aggregate several benefit packages into one during retirement years.
- Requiring couples to share equally Social Security benefits, even if one spouse does not work outside the home.
- Requiring companies to provide five years of health-care coverage to nonworking spouses after they are widowed or divorced.
- Raising the amount of income that a single-parent household can earn without paying taxes.
- Conducting a study of pay standards in the government to determine if there is sex-based discrimination.

As one of the primary sponsors of the bill, Pat Schroeder, said, this kind of legislation is necessary because "the real world no longer looks like a Norman Rockwell painting."

Welfare Reforms

When Congress decided not to support President Carter's

welfare reform package, it brought to an end a debate that had extended over three administrations. After years of investigation and discussion, Congress had decided that fundamental reform of the welfare system should not be built on a negative income tax system. President Reagan has proposed reducing spending for current programs, but no substitute for them. Since major reform is no longer on the agenda, some members of Congress have proposed rather modest reforms of current programs. Given the nation's budgetary problems, major reforms are not likely to be given serious attention in the next decade. Reform of existing programs may be the only hope that millions of poor Americans have for improved assistance. Some of the revisions in current programs under debate in Congress are examined below.

Altering the AFDC Program

In 1984 and 1985 the Omnibus Anti-Poverty Act was introduced into Congress by a bipartisan coalition of members. This bill proposes alterations in the ADFC program that have been debated and supported by many groups for years. The act would require the following five changes in the AFDC program.

First, all states would be required to meet a national minimum level of benefits for AFDC recipients. The minimum AFDC benefit, combined with food stamp benefits, would have to equal 65 percent of the poverty level for the family. In 1985 this would be a combined benefit of approximately $528 dollars ($396 for AFDC and $132 for food stamps) for a family of three. A majority of all the states would have to raise benefit levels under this proposal.

Second, the states would be required to extend AFDC benefits to all two-parent families living below the poverty level. Under current law, states may provide AFDC benefits to two-parent families where the father is unemployed or works fewer than 100 hours a month. Only twenty-two states and the District of Columbia have opted to participate in this program. The reform would extend the program to all states, but it would limit benefits to two-parent families to six months of any year. Families that became eligible for AFDC under this reform would also automatically qualify for Medicaid.

Third, deductions would be liberalized so that more working families could qualify for AFDC. Currently an AFDC recipient can deduct only $75 a month for work-related expenses. The reform would increase this to 20 percent of gross earnings or a maximum of $175. Recipients are currently allowed to deduct an additional $30 for twelve months, plus one-third of earnings for the first four months. The bill would change this to $50 and one-fourth with no time limit. Additionally, the child-care deduction would be capped at $320 a month, the EITC would no longer be counted as income, and the first $50 a month in unemployment compensation would be exempt.

Fourth, the asset limits would be raised to $2,250 from the current level of $1,000 (or less, at state option).

Fifth, to encourage the states to increase AFDC benefit levels, the federal government would assume a larger share of the total cost of the program. The federal government would reduce the states' share of the cost of increases in benefits by 30 percent.

The proposed changes would improve the financial circumstances of millions of poor families. This would be especially true in the South, where AFDC benefits tend to be very low and eligibility requirements strict. One study estimated that about one-third of AFDC families would receive substantially more benefits and some 300,000 families nationwide would be removed from poverty (Ways and Means 1985, 383). The estimated cost to all levels of government of all five changes would be $5.5 billion in 1986, rising to $10.5 billion in 1990. The cost would increase year by year as more recipients became aware of eligibility. The total cost of AFDC would increase from $16.3 billion to $21.8 billion in 1986.

Increased Housing Assistance

Far too few low-income families receive housing assistance. Only one in eight poor families receives housing assistance, including one in five AFDC families. Less than 40 percent of those families qualified for assistance by income receive it. Of those poor families with children who qualify as needy because they have incomes below the poverty level, or their income is below 50 percent of the area median, only one in six receives any type of housing assistance (Ways and Means 1985, 245). In 1985 this would mean that at least 4 million poor families with children were receiving no assistance.

Lack of housing assistance leaves millions of low-income families in inadequate or overcrowded housing and in undesirable neighborhoods. Additionally, it means that millions of low-income families must spend a disproportionate percentage of their total income on housing. Most studies conclude that housing costs in excess of 25 percent of income create serious financial burdens (Stone 1983). A recent study reported that 72 percent of all households earning $10,000 or less pay 25 percent or more of their total income for housing (Bureau of the Census 1981, table A-1). Many of these families are suffering from "shelter poverty." Their housing costs are so high they cannot afford many of the basic necessities. The Bureau of Labor Statistics has calculated the minimum budget required for nonshelter items. The BLS's figures show that a family of four with an income of $11,000 or less could not afford the basic necessities if they had any shelter costs (Stone 1983, 103–105).

There are currently five major federal housing programs that assist families with children. All of these programs are limited to families with incomes below the poverty level for their family size or with a median income below 50 percent of the area average. Recipients pay 30 percent of their adjusted income toward the cost of the housing unit. The rent subsidy programs pay the difference between this amount and the fair-market value of the unit. Usually the subsidy is paid directly to the landlord. In some cases the recipient receives a voucher that is redeemed by the landlord.

The first major program is public housing. In the early 1980s about half (480,000) of all public housing units in the United States were occupied by families with children (Burke 1984). The second program is "Section 8" rent subsidies in existing or modestly rehabilitated housing. About half of these units (330,000) serve families with children. The third is "Section 8" rent subsidies for new or substantially rehabilitated housing. Only about 20 percent of these units (104,000) are occupied by families with children. The fourth is "Section 236" subsidies to owners of low-income rental housing. The subsidies lower the operating costs of the units. About 40 percent, or 188,000, of these units are occupied by families with children. The last program is a rent subsidy program for some occupants of "Section 236" housing. About 74,000 families with children received these subsidies each year in the early 1980s. The five programs provide housing assistance to about 1.2 million low-income families with children.

The total cost of housing programs for all types of recipients was about $10 billion in 1984, a little more than 1 percent of the federal budget. As noted in Chapter 5, most of the other major Western industrial nations make a much larger commitment to housing assistance than does the United States. In countries such as Sweden and West Germany, some 40 percent of all families qualify for housing assistance; in Great Britain, about 20 percent of all families live in publicly owned housing. The European countries place a special emphasis on providing housing assistance to low-income families with children, especially those headed by a single parent. Widely used policies in these countries include extensive housing allowances, public housing, home purchase grants, rehabilitation loans, building and saving subsidies, and the promotion and subsidy of a nonprofit market.

The budgetary constraints facing the United States in the next decade make it unlikely that Congress will greatly increase funding for housing programs. It could, however, hold the cost of housing assistance constant and still increase assistance to low-income families by altering the tax deduction system used to subsidize home owners. Under current tax policies home owners can deduct all interest and taxes paid on their home or homes, regardless of their value. In 1983 deductions for interest and taxes cost the federal government $36.3 billion in lost revenues (Budget of the United States Government 1983, 5–76).

Housing assistance could be made much fairer by placing some limits on these tax deductions. An obvious option would be to limit the interest and tax deduction to some fixed dollar amount each year, and limit it to one home. Limiting the deduction to $25,000 in 1986, with a yearly adjustment for inflation, and limiting it to one home would increase federal tax revenues by several billion dollars a year. Even with this change, some 80 percent of all homeowners would still be able to deduct the full cost of the interest and tax expenses on their home. At current program costs, the $7 billion or so in new funds could be used to assist at least an additional one million low-income families with children.

Nutrition Programs

Meeting the nutritional needs of low-income people and families is relatively inexpensive. The total cost of all federal food programs was less than $20 billion in fiscal 1985. This includes the cost of the Food Stamp program, the nutrition program for Women, Infants, and Children (WIC), and all school meal programs. There is also considerable evidence that the various food programs have greatly reduced hunger and malnutrition in America since the mid-1960s (CBO 1980; Kotz 1979; Wellisch et al. 1983). However, notwithstanding the low cost of nutrition programs (especially compared to health-care costs), and the fact that the federal government spends huge amounts annually to store surplus (and perishable) farm commodities purchased from American farmers, the Reagan administration has tightened eligibility for food programs and reduced federal outlays (Ways and Means 1985, 521–25). These cutbacks occurred when the number of poor was increasing more dramatically than in any other period since the 1950s. Not surprisingly, there is evidence of substantial increases in the incidence of hunger and malnutrition in recent years (Select Committee on Hunger 1985).

There are several deficiencies in current food programs that should be remedied. First, the evidence indicates that a significant percentage of all food stamp families run out of food before the end of the month (Kotz 1979, 21). This problem is especially acute in families with children. Second, many families who fall on hard times cannot receive food stamps because they are disqualified by asset limits. Third, in rural areas some families cannot obtain food stamps because they live far from the distribution centers (Kotz 1979, 19). Fourth, funding for the WIC program is so deficient that the program serves only one-third of the women qualified by income. Fifth, despite increased poverty, school meal programs served almost 4 million fewer children in 1983 than in 1979 (Ways and Means 1985, 520).

Expanding the Food Stamp, WIC, and school meal programs to correct these problems would cost less than $4 billion a year. This is not a small sum, but food programs do put money back into the economy and they lower health-care expenditures. Thus, the net cost of food programs is much lower than outlays. Second, some nutrition problems could be met by a systematic distribution of government commodities. The

Reagan administration has distributed surplus commodities (especially cheese), but only episodically. A regular monthly distribution to low-income citizens would reduce government storage costs while helping millions of needy people.

Health Care

One of the most critical needs of low-income families is health-care assistance. The best estimates conclude that somewhere between 18 and 26 million Americans have no health insurance and another 37 million have only very limited coverage (CBO 1977, 12–13; Social Security Administration 1985, 33). Recent surveys reveal that more than half of all poor children live in families with no private or public health-care coverage (Ways and Means 1985, 327). Equally critical, a survey by the Alan Guttmacher Institute concluded that 25 percent of all women of the prime childbearing age (18–24) lack any type of medical coverage (*New York Times* 1985c, 7). This same survey found that 11 percent of all women who work full time, 16 percent working for an hourly wage, and 24 percent working for small companies have no health insurance.

Meeting health-care needs is relatively expensive, at least in the short run. Health care programs such as Medicaid are costly, but the evidence indicates that they have played a major role in reducing infant mortality rates and have improved the quality of health enjoyed by millions of recipients. The evidence is overwhelming that preventive health care pays for itself by reducing the incidence of serious, costly illness. It has been estimated, for example, that a complete prenatal treatment program costs about $600 (SCCYF 1984b, 27). By comparison, keeping a premature child in intensive care costs approximately $1,000 per day.

Health care could be extended to low-income families in a number of ways. One option would be to extend Medicaid coverage to all individuals living in households or families with incomes below the poverty level. Eligibility for Medicaid should be limited only by income, since linking eligibility to AFDC or SSI only forces people with medical needs to remain on the welfare rolls. A less attractive alternative would be to extend coverage to all children and pregnant women living in households or families with incomes below the poverty level.

Another approach that could be combined with expanded Medicaid coverage would be to increase the number of community health-care and migrant health-care centers. In 1985 there were 739 of these centers, serving about 5.5 million people a year. The centers provide free health care to persons at or below the poverty level, and reduced-cost care to other low-income patients. The centers cannot handle major medical problems and thus are not a total substitute for Medicaid. They can, however, take care of most of the health-care needs of recipients, and they are relatively cheap to finance. The centers in operation in 1985 were financed by payments from recipients, private insurance receipts, and subsidies by state and federal agencies.

Another option being discussed in some urban areas is for school districts to contract with health-maintenance organizations to handle the health-care needs of poor children. This option would provide a low-cost, comprehensive method of dealing with the health-care needs of children from low-income families.

Private industry will also have to do more. Employers should be required to provide employees and their families with decent health-care coverage. It would be financially advantageous for the federal government to subsidize HMOs that provide quality care at reasonable cost to employees of small companies and nonprofit entities.

Summary and Conclusions

The data presented in chapters 1 and 2 show the changes in

poverty demographics that have resulted in women and their dependent children becoming an increasingly large proportion of all the official poor in America. They indicate that the fastest growing type of family in America is that headed by a single woman. This type of family is five times as likely to be poor as a family headed by a married couple. As single-parent families increase, poverty—especially for children—increases very significantly. In the early 1980s both the number of poor children and the rate of poverty for children were the highest since the early 1960s. By 1984, 21 percent of all children were poor, making them the poorest age group in America. Currently almost half of all the poor and more than half of all poor children in America live in homes headed by single women.

The analysis in Chapter 2 revealed that the rate of poverty for female-headed families has always been high, and that the rate has not changed dramatically over the last fifteen years. What has changed is the number of female-headed families. As this type of family has increased as a proportion of all families, the high rate of poverty for such families has greatly increased the number of poor in female-headed households.

A number of factors have contributed to the increase in female-headed families, but the most important are rising rates of divorce, separation, and single parenting. All the evidence indicates that the number and proportion of all families headed by women will continue to grow. By the turn of the century, it can be expected that one out of four children will live in families headed by single women. The implications are obvious. Regardless of race, female-headed families tend to have low incomes (especially compared to male and two-parent families) and high rates of unemployment. Welfare benefits do not come close to compensating for the income deficiencies of poor female-headed families, and in the 1980s these benefits have been steadily reduced while the tax burden on low-income families has increased significantly. Some other types of social welfare programs, such as family planning services, have also been reduced and increasingly fail to reach the clients who need them most.

Statistical analysis reveals somewhat different correlates of poverty in black and white female-headed families. Black female-headed families often become the victims of poverty because of high rates of fertility, out-of-wedlock births, and divorce, combined with limited sources of income from employment, child support, and social welfare programs. The staggering rate of unemployment suffered by black males correlates strongly with the rate of poverty among black female-headed families. A causal relationship between the high rate of unemployment among black men and the high rates of divorce, abandonment, and out-of-wedlock births that cause much of the poverty in the black population seems apparent but needs to be more rigorously tested. The data suggest that white female-headed families fall into poverty because of increasing rates of divorce, high rates of unemployment, and limited sources of income, including inadequate social welfare services and child support.

Two major problems lie at the heart of increased rates of poverty among women. The first is the nation's continuing high rates of unemployment and subemployment for men and women. These problems are particularly severe for minority men. Second is the nation's failure to adapt its social policy to the changing role of women. This chapter has reviewed a range of nonwelfare policies and welfare reforms that could play a major role in addressing these two problems.

The evidence reviewed suggests that state and federal governments can play a significant role in lowering the unemployment rate. The states could make a major contribution by assuring that public school students receive an academically sound education. Better academic programs and standards in the nation's public schools would increase the employment prospects of millions of young people. Additionally, job-training and job-placement programs can be designed to meet the

needs of specific groups, such as minority teenagers and welfare mothers. The evidence clearly shows that teenagers,
young adults, and welfare mothers are job-oriented and that
they benefit significantly from well-designed programs. The
cost of substantially reducing unemployment among these
critical groups is quite reasonable, especially when discounted
by the cost of broken homes and increased crime and welfare
dependency.

Even women who work full time often earn less than they
should because of wage disparities and pay discrimination.
Issues of pay equity and sex discrimination still need considerable attention.

Much of the poverty and economic deprivation that women
and their dependent children suffer results from flaws in social
programs. Inadequate and poorly enforced child-support laws
create serious financial problems for millions of these families. Child-support statutes can be much better designed and
enforced. Lack of decent, affordable child care also imposes
hardships on millions of parents and children, often keeping
mothers from working or receiving the education or job training they need to become employable. Private employers and
public authorities can individually and in combination play a
significant role in ameliorating this problem. The lack of a
national maternity policy leaves mothers at the mercy of their
employers. A federal statute could establish guidelines for
employers, and a combined state–federal program could subsidize employees who cannot obtain the needed assistance from
their employer.

A number of federal policies could deal with many of the
problems that create financial hardships for female-headed
families. The federal commitment to family planning and sex
education needs to be greatly expanded. The Earned Income
Tax Credit can be amended in relatively minor ways to reduce
substantially the tax burden on low-income families. Federal
statutes could 1) improve the vestment rights of women who
move in and out of the job market because of family responsi-

bilities; 2) increase the IRA contribution of a nonworking spouse; 3) require that Social Security benefits be equally shared by a couple, regardless of the work record of each partner; and 4) obligate employers to cover the health-care needs of nonworking spouses for a set number of years after they are widowed or divorced.

The nation's major welfare programs are very badly flawed and in serious need of revision. Most obviously, the AFDC program should be extended to all poor families, regardless of composition, and there should be a national minimum benefit level. These two changes would improve the program substantially without greatly raising costs. The nation also needs to accept responsibility for improving housing assistance, nutrition programs, and health care.

These reforms individually and in combination could play a role in greatly reducing the current rate of poverty among women and children. They would not be cheap, but they could be implemented for reasonable costs. Well-designed programs that substantially reduced poverty among women and children would in the long run pay for themselves many times over.

The federal government has a proven record of reducing poverty when it decides to do so. In 1959, 35.2 percent of all Americans age 65 and over lived in poverty. By 1984 the poverty rate for the aged was 12.4 percent. The rate dropped significantly because expenditures for Social Security were increased and pegged to inflation, while most of the medical needs of the aged were covered by Medicare and Medicaid. The aged have learned the value of government assistance and are a well-organized lobby. By 1985 over 30 percent of the total federal budget consisted of expenditures for the aged. By contrast, less than 10 percent of the budget is devoted to programs for low-income families with children. Both the public and the private sector need to recognize the gravity of the problem, and each needs to do a great deal more to come to grips with it. At stake is the future of our society.

References

Alford, R. 1975. "Paradigms of Relations Between State and Society."
In *Stress and Contradiction in Modern Capitalism*, ed. L. Lindbery et
al. Lexington, Mass.: Lexington Books.

Bahr, S. J. 1979. "The Effects of Welfare on Marital Stability and Remarriage." *Journal of Marriage and the Family* 41 (August): 533-60.

Bane, M. J. 1976. *Here to Stay: American Families in the Twentieth Century*. New York: Basic Books.

Bane, M. J., and Ellwood, D. T. 1983. "The Dynamics of Dependency:
The Routes to Self-Sufficiency." Cambridge, Mass.: Urban Systems
Research and Engineering.

Becker, G. S. 1981. *A Treatise on the Family*. Cambridge: Harvard University Press.

Beckerman, W. 1979. "The Impact of Income Maintenance Payments on
Poverty in Britain, 1975." *The Economic Journal* (June): 261-79.

Beller, A. H. 1980. "The Effect of Economic Conditions on the Success
of Equal Employment Opportunity Laws." *The Review of Economics
and Statistics* 62 (August).

—————. 1982. "Occupational Segregation by Sex: Determinants and
Changes." *The Journal of Human Resources* 17, 3 (Summer).

Bergman, B. 1974. "Occupational Segregation, Wages and Profits When Employers Discriminate by Race or Sex." *Eastern Economic Journal* 1 (April): 103–10.

Berrueta-Clement, J. R. et al. 1984. *Changed Lives: The Effects of the Perry Preschool Program on Youths Through Age 19.* Ypsilanti, Mich.: High Scope Educational Research Foundation.

Bianchi, S., and Farley, R. 1979. "Racial Differences in Family Living Arrangements and Economic Well-Being: An Analysis of Recent Trends." *Journal of Marriage and the Family* 41 (August): 537–51.

Brown, Bernard. 1977. "Long-Term Gains from Early Intervention: An Overview of Current Research." Paper presented at the 1977 Annual Meeting of the American Association for the Advancement of Sciences, Denver.

Budget of the United States Government: Fiscal Year 1983. Washington, D.C.: GPO.

Bumpass, L., and Rindfuss, R. R. 1979. "Children and the Experience of Marital Disruption." *American Journal of Sociology* 85 (July): 49–65.

Bureau of the Census. 1976. "Number, Timing, and Duration of Marriages and Divorce in the United States: June 1975." *Current Population Reports.* Series P-20, no. 297. Washington, D.C.: GPO.

—————. 1979. *Statistical Abstract of the United States 1979.* 100th ed. Washington, D.C.: GPO.

—————. 1980a. "Child Support and Alimony: 1978." *Current Population Reports.* Special Studies Series P-23, no. 106, Advance Report. Washington, D.C.: GPO.

—————. 1980b. *Statistical Abstract of the United States 1980.* 101st ed. Washington, D.C.: GPO.

—————. 1981a. "Characteristics of Households and Persons Receiving Noncash Benefits." *Current Population Reports.* Series P-32, no. 110. Washington, D.C.: GPO.

—————. 1981b. "Current Housing Reports, Annual Housing Survey: 1980, Part C, Financial Characteristics of the Housing Inventory, U.S. Regions." Series H15–80. Washington, D.C.: GPO.

—————. 1981c. *Statistical Abstract of the United States 1981.* 102d ed. Washington, D.C.: GPO.

—————. 1982a. "Child Care Arrangements of Working Mothers: June, 1982." *Current Population Reports.* Series P-23, no. 129. Washington, D.C.: GPO.

—————. 1982b. "Fertility of American Women: June 1981." *Current Population Reports.* Series P-20, no. 369. Washington, D.C.: GPO.

—————. 1982c. "Population Profiles of the United States: 1981." *Current Population Reports.* Series P-20, no. 374. Washington, D.C.: GPO.

————. 1984a. "Economic Characteristics of Households in the United States: First Quarter 1984." *Current Population Reports*. Series P-70, no. 3. Washington, D.C.: GPO.

————. 1985a. "Money Income and Poverty Status of Families and Persons in the United States: 1984." *Current Population Reports*. Series P-60, no. 149. Washington, D.C.: GPO.

————. 1985b. *Statistical Abstract of the United States: 1984*. 104th ed. Washington, D.C.: GPO.

————. 1985c. "Economic Characteristics of Households in the United States: First Quarter, 1984." *Current Population Reports*. Series P-70, no. 3. Washington, D.C.: GPO.

Burke, V. 1984. "Cash and Non-Cash Benefits for Persons with Limited Income: Eligibility Rules, Recipient and Expenditure Data: FY 1981–83." Congressional Research Service, Report no. 84–99.

Burke, V., Gabe, T., Rimkunas, R., and Griffith, J. 1985. *Hispanic Children in Poverty*. Washington, D.C.: Congressional Research Service, Report no. 85–170.

Burlage, D. 1978. "Divorced and Separated Mothers: Combining the Responsibilities of Breadwinning and Child Rearing." Ph.D. dissertation, Harvard University.

Burnham, W. D. 1980. "American Politics in the 1980s." *Dissent* (Spring): 152–57.

Burstein, P. 1979. "Equal Employment Opportunity Legislation and the Income of Women and Nonwhites." *American Sociological Review* 44 (June): 367–91.

Business Week. 1985. "The Forgotten Americans." September 2, pp. 50–55.

Carlson, E., and Stinson, K. 1982. "Motherhood, Marriage Timing, and Marital Stability: A Research Note." *Social Forces* 61 (September): 258–67.

Center for the Study of Social Policy. 1984. "Working Female-Headed Families in Poverty: Three Studies of Low-Income Families Affected by the AFDC Policy Changes in 1981." Washington, D.C.

Chafe, W. H. 1972. *The American Woman: Her Changing Social, Economic and Political Role, 1920–1970*. New York: Oxford University Press.

Chafetz, J. S. 1984., *Sex and Advantage: A Comparative Macro-Structural Theory of Sex Stratification*. Totowa, N.J.: Rowman & Allanheld.

Cherlin, A. 1980. "Postponing Marriage: The Influence of Young Women's Work Expectations." *Journal of Marriage and the Family*.42 (May): 355–65.

————. 1981. *Marriage, Divorce, and Remarriage*. Cambridge: Harvard University Press.

Children's Defense Fund. 1984. "The Deficit Reduction Act of 1984." Washington, D.C.

Cicirelli, V. G. et al. 1977. *The Impact of Head Start: An Evaluation of the Effects of Head Start on Children's Cognitive and Affective Development*. Ohio University, Westinghouse Learning Corporation.

Citizens' Board of Inquiry into Hunger and Malnutrition in the United States. 1968. *Hunger, USA*. Boston: Beacon.

Clayton, R. R., and Voss, H. L. 1977. "Shacking Up: Cohabitation in the 1970s." *Journal of Marriage and the Family* 39 (May): 273–83.

Cocoran, M., and Duncan, G. 1979. "Work History, Labor Force Attachment, and Earnings Differences Between Races and Sexes." *Journal of Human Resources* 14 (Winter): 3–20.

Cole, S., Danziger, S., Danziger, S., and Piliavin, I. 1983. "Poverty and Welfare Recipiency after OBRA: Some Preliminary Evidence from Wisconsin." Madison: University of Wisconsin, Institute for Research on Poverty.

Commission of the European Communities. 1981. *Final Report from the Commissioners to the Council on the First Programme of Pilot Scheme and Studies to Combat Poverty*. Brussels.

——————. 1982. *One-Parent Families and Poverty in the EEC*. Copenhagen.

Committee on Ways and Means. 1985. *Children in Poverty*. U.S. House of Representatives, 99th Congress, 1st Session. Washington, D.C.: GPO.

Congressional Budget Office. 1977a. *Catastrophies Health Insurance*. Washington, D.C.: GPO.

——————. 1977b. *The Food Stamp Program: Income or Food Supplementative?* Washington, D.C.: GPO.

——————. 1980. *Feeding Children: Federal Child Nutrition Policies in the 1980s*. Washington, D.C.: GPO.

——————. 1983. "Major Legislative Changes in Human Resources Programs since January 1981." Staff memorandum, August.

Congressional Quarterly Weekly Report. 1982. "For the Poor, a Wait for Better Housing." (December 4).

Cooney, R. S. 1979. "Demographic Components of Growth in White, Black and Puerto Rican Female-Headed Families: Comparison of the Cutright and Ross Sawhill Methodologies." *Social Research* 8 (June): 144–58.

Cottingham, C., ed. 1982. *Race, Poverty, and the Urban Underclass*. Lexington, Mass.: Lexington Books.

Cramer, J. C. 1980. "Fertility and Female Employment." *American Sociological Review* 47 (August): 556–67.

Cutright, P. 1974. "Components of Change in the Number of Female Family Heads Aged 15–44: U.S., 1940–70." *Journal of Marriage and the Family* 36 (November): 714–21.

Danziger, S. 1981. "Post-Program Changes in the Lives of AFDC Supported Work Participants: A Quantitative Assessment." *Journal of*

Human Resources 16 (April).

──────. 1982. "Children in Poverty: The Truly Needy Who Fall Through the Safety Net." *Children and Youth Services*, 35–51.

──────. 1984. "The Impact of the Reagan Budget Cuts on Working Welfare Mothers in Wisconsin." *Institute for Research on Poverty* (November): 763–84.

Danziger, S., and Haveman, R. 1981. "The Reagan Administration's Budget Cuts: Their Impact on the Poor," *Challenge* 24 (May-June): 5–13.

Department of Labor. 1984. "Analysis of Job Training, Longitudinal Survey with Turn Around Data: JTPA Title II-A (October 1983-March 1984)."

Downes, B. T. 1968. "Social and Political Characteristics of Riot Cities: A Comparative Study." *Social Science Quarterly* 49 (December): 509–20.

Duvall, L. J., Gondreau, D. W., and Marsh, R. E. 1982. "Aid to Families with Dependent Children: Characteristics of Recipients in 1979." *Social Security Bulletin* 45, 4 (April): 1, 6.

Easterlin, R. 1980. *Birth and Fortune: The Impact of Numbers on Personal Wealth.* New York: Basic Books.

Ellwood, D. T., and Bane, M. J. 1984. "The Impact of AFDC on Family Structure and Living Arrangements." Unpublished paper.

Espenshade, T. J. 1979. "The Economic Consequences of Divorce." *Journal of Marriage and the Family* 41 (August): 615–25.

Evanson, E. 1984. "Employment Programs for the Poor: Government in the Labor Market." *Focus* 7, 3 (Fall): 1–7.

Feagin, J. R. 1975. *Subordinating the Poor: Welfare and American Beliefs.* Englewood Cliffs, N.J.: Prentice-Hall.

Fester, D., Gottschalk, P., and Jakubson, G. 1984. "Impact of OBRA on AFDC Recipients in Wisconsin." Institute for Research on Poverty. Discussion paper no. 763–84 (November).

Finer, M. et al. 1974. *Report on the Committee on One-Parent Families.* London: Her Majesty's Stationery Office.

Flora, P., and Heidenheimer, A. J., eds. 1981. *The Development of Welfare States in Europe and America.* New Brunswick, N.J: Transaction.

Forest, J. D., Hermalin, A. I., and Henshaw, S. K. 1981. "The Impact of Family Planning Clinic Programs on Adolescent Pregnancy." *Family Planning Perspective* 13, 3.

Freeman, J. 1975. *The Politics of Women's Liberation.* New York: Longman.

Fuchs, V. 1981. *How We Live.* Cambridge: Harvard University Press.

Furniss, N., and Mitchell, N. 1984. "Social Welfare Provisions in Western Europe: Current Status and Future Possibilities." In *Public Policy and Social Institutions*, ed. H. Rodgers. Greenwich, Conn.: JAI Press.

Furniss, N., and Tilton, T. 1979. *The Case for the Welfare State: From Social Security to Social Equality.* Bloomington: Indiana University Press.

Furstenberg, F. F., Jr. 1976. *Unplanned Parenthood: The Social Consequences of Teenage Childbearing.* New York: Free Press.

Furstenberg, F. F., Jr., Lincoln, R., and Menken, J. 1981. *Teenage Sexuality, Pregnancy, and Childbearing.* Philadelphia: University of Pennsylvania Press.

Garkinkel, I., and Uhr, E. 1984. "A New Approach to Child Support." *The Public Interest* 75 (Spring): 111–22.

General Accounting Office. 1980. *Better Management and More Resources Needed to Strengthen Federal Efforts to Improve Pregnancy Outcomes.* Washington, D.C.: GPO.

Gilder, George. 1981. *Wealth and Poverty.* New York: Bantam.

Ginsburg, H. 1983. *Full Employment and Public Policy: The United States and Sweden.* Lexington, Mass: Lexington Books.

Glick, P. C., and Spanier, G. B. 1980. "Married and Unmarried Cohabitation in the United States." *Journal of Marriage and the Family* 42 (February): 19–30.

Gold, M. E. 1983. *A Dialogue on Comparable Worth.* New York: ILR Press, New York State School of Industrial and Labor Relations, Cornell University.

Gottschalk, P. 1981. "Transfer Scenarios and Projections of Poverty into the 1980s." *Journal of Human Resources* 16, 41–60.

Guttentag, M., and Secord, P. 1983. *Too Many Women: The Sex Ratio Question.* Beverly Hills: Sage.

Hahn, L. H., and Feagin, J. R. 1970. "Rank-and-File Versus Congressional Perceptions of Ghetto Riots." *Social Science Quarterly* 51 (September): 361–73.

Hannan, M. T., Tuma, N. B., and Groeneveld, P. 1977. "Income and Marital Events: Evidence from the Income Maintenance Experiment." *American Journal of Sociology* 82 (May): 1186–1211.

Headey, B. 1978. *Housing Policy in the Developed Economy: The United Kingdom, Sweden, and the United States.* London: Croom Helm.

Hofferth, S., and Moore, K. 1979. "Early Childbearing and Later Economic Well-being." *American Sociological Review* 44 (October): 784–815.

Hollister, R. G., Kemper, P., and Maynard, R. A., eds. 1984. *The National Supported Work Demonstration.* Madison: University of Wisconsin Press.

Houston *Chronicle.* 1985a. "Many States Now Offer Work Fare." October 13, p. 24.

Houston *Chronicle.* 1985b. "Schools Failing U.S. Business, Report Charges." September 6, p. 18.

Human Resources Administration. 1983. "Effects of Federal Budget

Cutbacks on Employed ADC Parents.'' New York: City of New York.

Hutchens, R. 1984. ''Changing the AFDC Program: The Effects of the Omnibus Budget Reconciliation Act of 1981.'' *Institute For Research on Poverty*, Discussion Paper no. 764-84 (December).

Institute for Research on Poverty. 1985. ''Measuring the Effects of the Reagan Welfare Changes on the Work Effort and Well-Being of Single Parents.'' *Focus* 8, 1: 1-5.

Jackson, J. J. 1973. ''Black Women in a Racist Society.'' In *Racism and Mental Health*, ed. C. V. Willie, B. M. Kramer, and B. S. Brown. Pittsburgh: University of Pittsburgh Press.

Johansen, E. 1984. *Comparable Worth: The Myth and the Movement.* Boulder, Colo.: Westview Press.

Jones, E. F., Forest, J. D., Goldman, N., Henshaw, S. K., Lincoln, R., Rosoff, J., Wehoff, C. F., and Wolf, D. 1985. ''Teenage Pregnancy in Developed Countries: Determinants and Policy Implications.'' *Family Planning Perspectives* 17 (March April): 53-63.

Kamerman, S. B. 1984. ''Women, Children and Poverty: Public Policies and Female-headed Families in Industrialized Countries.'' *Signs: Journal of Women in Culture and Society* 10, 21: 249-71.

Kamerman, S. B., and Kahn, A. J. 1981. *Child Care, Family Benefits, and Working Parents.* New York: Columbia University Press.

————. 1983. ''Child Support: Some International Developments.'' In *Parental Support Obligations*, ed. J. Cassetty. Lexington, Mass.: Lexington Books.

Kessler-Harris, A. 1982. *Out to Work—A History of Wage-Earning Women in the United States.* New York: Oxford University Press.

Kimmich, M. 1984. ''Children's Services in the Reagan Era.'' Washington, D.C.: Urban Institute.

King, A. G. 1978. ''Labor Market Racial Discrimination Against Black Women.'' *The Review of Black Political Economy* 8, 4 (Summer).

Kobrin, KF. E. 1973. ''Household Headship and Its Changes in the United States, 1940-1960, 1970.'' *Journal of the American Statistical Association* 68 (December): 793-800.

Kotz, N. 1971. Let Them Eat Promises: *The Politics of Hunger in America.* New York: Doubleday.

————. 1979. *Hunger in America: The Federal Response.* New York: Field Foundation.

Lantz, H., Martin, S., and O'Hara, M. 1977. ''The Changing American Family from the Preindustrial to the Industrial Period: A Final Report.'' *American Sociological Review* 42 (June): 406-21.

Lasch, K. C. 1980. ''Life in the Therapeutic State.'' *New York Review of Books* 27 (June 12): 24-32.

Leichter, H. M. 1979. *A Comparative Approach to Policy Analysis: Health Care Policy in Four Nations.* New York: Cambridge University Press.

Leichter, H. M., and Rodgers, H. R. Jr. 1984. *American Public Policy in a Comparative Context*. New York: McGraw-Hill.

Leman, C. 1977. "Patterns of Policy Development: Social Security in the United States and Canada." *Public Policy* 25 (Spring): 261–91.

Levitan, S., Rein, M., and Marwick, D. 1972. *Work and Welfare Go Together*. Baltimore: Johns Hopkins Press.

Levy, F. 1980. "Labor Force Dynamics and the Distribution of Employability." Washington, D.C.: Urban Institute.

Lloyd, C. B., and Niemi, B. T. 1979. *The Economics of Sex Differentials*. New York: Columbia University Press.

McGuire, C. C. 1981. *International Housing Policies: A Comparative Analysis*. Lexington, Mass.: Lexington Books.

Maller, C. et al. 1984. *The Lasting Impact of Job Corps Participation*. Princeton, N.J.: Mathematica.

Mann, A. J. 1977. "A Review of Head Start Research since 1969." Paper presented at the 1977 Annual Meeting of the American Association for the Advancement of Science, Denver.

Manpower Demonstration Research Corp. 1985. "Job Start: Report One." New York: MDRC Corp.

Milgram, G. 1984. "Trends in Funding and Number of Households in HUD-Assisted Housing: Fiscal Years 1974–1984." *Budget of the U.S. Government, Fiscal Year 1986, Appendix*. Washington, D.C.: GPO.

Miller, A. C. 1975. "Health Care of Children and Youth in America." *American Journal of Public Health* 65 (April): 353–58.

Moles, O. C. 1979. "Public Welfare Payments and Marital Disolution: A Review of Recent Studies." In *Divorce and Separation: Context, Causes, and Consequences*, ed. George Levinger and Oliver C. Moles New York: Basic Books.

Moore, K., and Burt, M. 1981. *Teenage Childbearing and Welfare: Policy Perspectives on Sexual Activity, Pregnancy, and Public Dependency*. Washington, D.C.: Urban Institute.

Moore, K., and Caldwell, S. 1976. *Out-of-Wedlock Pregnancy and Childbearing*. Washington, D.C.: Urban Institute.

————. 1977. "The Effect of Government Policies on Out-of-Wedlock Sex and Pregnancy." *Family Planning Perspective* 9, 1 (July August).

Moore, K., and Waite, L. 1981. "Marital Dissolution, Early Motherhood and Early Marriage." *Social Forces* 60 (September): 20–40.

Moscovice, I., and Craig, W. 1983. "The Impact of Federal Cutbacks on Working AFDC Recipients in Minnesota." University of Minnesota, (December).

Murphy, I. L. 1973. *Public Policy on the Status of Women*. Lexington, Mass.: Heath.

Murray, C. 1984. *Losing Ground: American Social Policy*. New York: Basic Books.

National Black Child Development Institute. 1983. *The Status of Black Children in 1980: A Response to the President's Budget for Fiscal Year 1983*. Washington, D.C.

National Center for Health Statistics. 1982. "Advance Report of Final Mortality Statistics Report." *Monthly Vital Statistics Report* 31, 6, Supplement.

National Committee on Pay Equity. 1984. *Who's Working for Working Women*. Washington, D.C.: GPO.

National Forum Foundation. 1985. *Child Support Enforcement: Unequal Protection under the Law*. Washington, D.C.

New York Times. 1985a. "Cost of Care of 'Latchkey Children' Debated." August 7: 1, 12.

New York Times. 1985b. "More Corporation Are Offering Child Care." June 21: 25.

New York Times. 1985c. "Survey Reveals Lack of Health Care." October 7: 7.

Oaxaca, R. 1973. "Male-Female Wage Differentials in Urban Labor Markets." *International Economic Review* 14: 693–709.

Office of Economic Research. 1981. *U.S. Economic Performance in a Global Perspective*. New York: New York Stock Exchange.

OECD. 1976. *Public Expenditures on Income Maintenance Programmes*. Paris.

Pearce, D. 1978. "The Feminization of Poverty: Women, Work and Welfare." *Urban and Social Change Review*.

Perlman, S. 1984. *Nobody's Baby: The Politics of Adolescent Pregnancy*. Doctoral dissertation, The Florence Heller School for Advanced Studies in Social Welfare, Brandeis University.

Piven, F. F., and Cloward, R. A. 1979. *Poor People's Movements: Why They Succeed, How They Fail*. New York: Random House.

Piven, F. F., and Cloward, R. A. 1971. *Regulating the Poor: The Functions of Public Welfare*. New York: Vintage Books.

Polachek, S. W. 1979. "Occupational Segregation among Women: Theory, Evidence, and a Prognosis." In *Women in the Labor Market*, ed. Cynthia B. Lloyd. New York: Columbia University Press.

Remick, H., ed. 1981. *Comparable Worth and Wage Discrimination*. Philadelphia: Temple University Press.

Rivlin, A. M. 1984. "Helping the Poor." In *Economic Choices: 1984*, ed. A. M. Rivlin. Washington, D.C.: Brookings Institution.

Rodgers, H. R., Jr. 1978. "Hiding Versus Ending Poverty." *Politics and Society* 8: 253–66.

————. 1979. *Poverty Amid Plenty: A Political and Economic Analysis*. Reading, Mass.: Addison-Wesley.

————. 1982. *The Cost of Human Neglect: America's Welfare Failure*. Armonk, N.Y.: M.E. Sharpe.

Roemer, M. 1977. *Comparative National Policies on Health Care*. New

York: Marcel Dekker.

Rosengren, B. 1973. *Pre-School in Sweden*. Stockholm: Swedish Institute.

Ross, H. L., and Sawhill, I. 1975. *Time of Transition: The Growth of Families Headed by Women*. Washington, D.C.: Urban Institute.

Ross, S. C. 1973. *The Rights of Women*. New York: Avon Books.

Rytina, N. F. 1982. "Tenure as a Factor in the Male-Female Earnings Gap." *Monthly Labor Review* (April): 32–34.

Scharf, K. R. 1979. "Teenage Pregnancy: Why the Epidemic?" *Working Papers for a New Society* 6 (March April).

Select Committee on Children, Youth, and Families. 1983a. "Children, Youth and Families: Beginning the Assessment." House of Representatives, 98th Congress, 1st Session. Washington, D.C.: GPO.

——————. 1983b. "U.S. Children and Their Families: 1983: Current Conditions and Recent Trends." 98th Congress, 1st Session. Washington, D.C.: GPO.

——————. 1984a. *Demographic and Social Trends: Implications for Federal Support of Dependent-Care Service for Children and the Elderly*. CP 98–767, 98th Congress, 1st Session. Washington, D.C.: GPO.

——————. 1984b. *Children, Youth and Families: 1983*. 98–1179, 98th Congress, 2d Session. Washington, D.C.: GPO.

——————. 1984c. *Federal Programs Affecting Children*. 98–223, 98th Congress, 1st Session. Washington, D.C.: GPO.

——————. 1984d. "Teenagers in Crisis: Issues and Programs." House of Representatives, 98th Congress. Washington, D.C.: GPO.

Select Committee on Hunger (House). 1985. *The Effects of Hunger on Infant and Child Health in the U.S.* Washington, D.C.: GPO.

Sexton, P. 1977. *Women and Work*. Research and Development Corporation. Washington, D.C.: Department of Labor, Employment and Training Administration.

Silver, G. A. 1978. *Child Health: America's Future*. Germantown, Md.: Aspen Systems Corp.

Simanis, J. G., and Coleman, J. R. 1980. "Health Care Expenditures in Nine Industrial Countries." *Social Security Bulletin* 43 (January): 3–8.

Smith, R. E., ed. 1979. *The Subtle Revolution: Women at Work*. Washington, D.C.: Urban Institute.

Smith-Loving, L., and Tickamyer, A. 1978. "Nonrecursive Models of Labor Force Participation, Fertility Behavior, and Sex Role Attitudes." *American Sociological Review* 43 (August): 541–56.

Smith-Loving, L., and Tickamyer, A. 1982. "Models of Fertility and Women's Work (Comment on Cramer, *ASR*, April 1980)." *American Sociological Review* 47 (August): 561–66.

Smolensky, E. 1985. "Is a Golden Age in Poverty Policy Right Around the Corner?'' *Focus* 8 (Spring): 9–11.

Social Security Administration. 1982. *1979 Recipient Characteristics Study, Part 2: Financial Circumstances of AFDC Families.* Washington, D.C.: GPO.

————. 1983. ''Monthly Benefit Statistics.'' No. 11. Washington, D.C.: GPO.

————. 1985. *Social Security Bulletin* 48, 7 (July). Washington, D.C.: GPO.

Steiner, G. Y. 1976. *The Children's Cause.* Washington, D.C.: Brookings Institution.

Stone, M. 1983. ''Housing and the Economic Crisis.'' In *America's Housing Crisis: What Is To Be Done?* ed. C. Hartman. Boston: Routledge and Kegan Paul.

Subcommittee on Public Assistance (Senate). 1980. *Statistical Data Reflected to Public Assistance Programs.* CP96–30, 96th Congress, 2d Session.

Sulzbach, W. 1947. *German Experience with Social Insurance.* New York: National Industrial Conference Board.

Suter, L., and Miller, H. 1973. ''Income Differences Between Men and Career Women.'' *American Journal of Sociology* 78 (January): 962–74.

Sweet, J. A. 1972. ''The Living Arrangements of Separated, Widowed, and Divorced Mothers.'' *Demography* 9 (February): 143–57.

Townsend, P. 1979. *Poverty in the United Kingdom.* Los Angeles: University of California Press.

Trieman, D. J., and Hartmann, H. I., eds. 1981. *Women, Work, and Wages: Equal Pay for Jobs of Equal Value.* Washington, D.C.: National Academy Press.

U.S. Commission on Civil Rights. 1982. *Unemployment and Underemployment among Blacks, Hispanics, and Women.* Washington, D.C.: GPO.

————. 1983. *A Growing Crisis: Disadvantaged Women and Their Children.* No. 78. Washington, D.C.: GPO.

Vining, D. R. 1983. ''Illegitimacy and Public Policy.'' *Population and Development Review* 9 (March).

Vinovskis, M. A. 1981. ''An 'Epidemic' of Adolescent Pregnancy? Some Historical Considerations.'' *Journal of Family History* 6, 2 (Summer).

Wagner, L. M., and Wagner, M. 1976. *The Danish National Child Care System.* Boulder, Colo.: Westview.

Ways and Means. *See* Committee on Ways and Means.

Weatherley, R. 1985. ''Adolescent Pregnancy; Patriachy and the Politics of Transgression.'' Paper presented at the Annual Meeting of the Western Political Science Association, Las Vegas.

Weitzman, L. J. 1980. ''The Economics of Divorce: Social and Economic Consequences of Property, Alimony and Child Support Awards." *UCLA Law Review* 28, 6.

Wellisch, C. et al. 1983. "The National Evaluation of School Nutrition Programs: Final Report." Santa Monica, Calif.: System Development Corporation 1 (April): 4–8.

Wertheimer, R. F., and Moore, K. A. 1982. "Teenage Childbearing: Public Sector Costs—Final Report." Washington, D.C.: Urban Institute.

Wilensky, H. 1975. *The Welfare State and Equality*. Berkeley: University of California Press.

Wolf, W., and Fligstein, N. 1979. "Sex and Authority in the Workplace: Causes of Sexual Inequality." *American Sociological Review* 44, 2 (April).

Yavis, J. 1982. *The Head Start Program—History, Legislation, Issues and Funding—1964–1982*. Congressional Research Service Report No. 82–93 EPW. May.

Young, D. R., and Nelson, R. R., eds. 1973. *Public Policy for Day Care of Young Children*. Lexington, Mass.: Lexington Books.

Index

Abortion rates, 92, 93, 94, 123

Advance maintenance payments. *See* Child support

Aid to Dependent Children (ADC), 57

Aid to Families with Dependent Children (AFDC): amendment to (1961), 60, 65; benefits, 74–78; costs of, 71; and education, 83–86; and family allowances, 116; and family planning, 92–94; and health care, 86–87; and housing, 87–89; need for extension of, 149; and nutrition, 90–92; overview of, 70–74; problems with, 78–83; proposed changes to, 138–40; recipients, 14, 71, 74; renamed, 57; state variations in, 74–75; UF (Unemployed Father) program, 70–71, 83; and workfare, 131–32. *See also* Cash-assistance programs

Alaska, 74–75

Austria, 102

Belgium, 99

Birth rates, 39–41

Blacks: child support rates, 43; divorce rates, 39, 41, 51, 52; fertility rates, 51; income rates, 46; in female-headed households, 10; poverty among, 10, 17, 19, 22, 24, 25, 27, 29, 31, 35, 53, 147; and single parenting, 40, 41–42; 50–51; unemployment among, 42, 43, 45, 51–52, 128, 131, 147

Buffalo, 127

California, 74, 132

Canada, 99

Carter administration, 113, 130–31

Cash-assistance programs, 58, 65, 68. *See also* Aid to Families with Dependent Children; Supplemental Security Income

About the Author

HARRELL R. RODGERS, Jr., is Professor of Political Science at the University of Houston. He is a policy analyst specializing in poverty and welfare policy, civil rights, and political economics.

Rodgers is the author or co-author of fifteen books and numerous articles in the fields of policy analysis, law and social change, and American politics, and has won three professional awards for his work on these subjects. Among his most recent works are *The Cost of Human Neglect: America's Welfare Failure* (1982) and (with Michael Harrington) *Unfinished Democracy*.